THE APPLICATION OF THE RORSCHACH TEST TO YOUNG CHILDREN

UNIVERSITY OF MINNESOTA
THE INSTITUTE OF CHILD WELFARE
MONOGRAPH SERIES NO. XXIII

The Application of the Rorschach Test to Young Children

BY

MARY FORD

ASSOCIATE PROFESSOR OF CHILD DEVELOPMENT AND FAMILY RELATIONSHIPS, NEW YORK STATE COLLEGE OF HOME ECONOMICS, CORNELL UNIVERSITY

GREENWOOD PRESS, PUBLISHERS
WESTPORT, CONNECTICUT

Library of Congress Cataloging in Publication Data

Ford, Mary Elizabeth Nestlerode, 1907-
The application of the Rorschach test to young children.

Reprint of the ed. published by University of Minnesota Press, Minneapolis, which was issued as no. 23 of the University of Minnesota, Institute of Child Welfare monograph series.
Bibliography: p.
Includes index.
1. Rorschach test. 2. Child study. I. Title. II. Series: Minnesota. University. Institute of Child Development and Welfare. Monograph series ; no. 23.
BF698.8.R5F67 1975 155.4'18 70-141545
ISBN 0-8371-5892-3

Originally published in 1946 by the University of Minnesota Press, Minneapolis

Reprinted with the permission of The University of Minnesota Press

Reprinted by Greenwood Press,
a division of Williamhouse-Regency Inc.

First Greenwood Reprinting 1975
Second Greenwood Reprinting 1976

Library of Congress Catalog Card Number 70-141545

ISBN 0-8371-5892-3

Printed in the United States of America

FOREWORD

One of the most widely used modern instruments for evaluating the personality of older children and adults, particularly those who deviate, is the Rorschach Inkblot Test. In the twenty years since its first appearance, interest in the Rorschach Test as a clinical instrument has grown beyond all expectation. The large number of experimental studies in which it has been used and the many books written about it bear testimony to this interest. Although attempts have been made to apply the Rorschach techniques to younger children, as yet but few detailed analyses of the results obtained by its use are available for children of preschool age.

In this study Dr. Ford sets herself four major aims: (1) the refinement of administrative procedures and simplification of the instructions to make them meaningful to young children; (2) the study of the variations in test determinants with chronological age, mental age, and sex, as a basis for a future standardization of the test for young children; (3) the study of the reliability of the test determinants at the preschool level; and (4) the checking of the validity of specific claims made by Rorschach workers as to the meaning of the various test determinants. Children from three to eight years of age were used. The children were much interested and maintained high motivation throughout the tests.

The results obtained by Dr. Ford show that some determinants increase significantly with chronological age, others show only small increases, and still others show decrease or no variation. The content of the responses is but slightly related to age except that with increase in age a wider range of content appears. No marked sex differences were found, i.e., the variation within a sex group is greater than the slight variation between groups. The test-retest reliabilities vary with the determinants; some are small and some very significant.

Dr. Ford stresses the need of careful standardization and norms and feels that her results offer some basis for the development of such standards. She also suggests the importance of standardizing a simple trial blot so that pretest conditions may be similar for all subjects. A number of other suggestions are made for the future study of the Rorschach on young children. The Appendixes give a detailed description of the items within the content classifications and sample records of three children, aged three, five, and seven years. In addition there are a glossary of definitions of the Rorschach terminology used in the study and an extensive bibliography.

Without question this monograph constitutes an important addition to the scientific literature on the Rorschach Test and on the behavior of young children. The results are significant contributions to the study of the personality of children in their own right, and if the suggestions and implications made are carried through to completion, very substantial additions to our knowledge of children will ensue.

John E. Anderson
Director, Institute of Child Welfare
University of Minnesota

ACKNOWLEDGMENTS

The writer wishes to express her appreciation to the many persons and institutions whose cooperation has made this study possible: to the children and their teachers of the nursery school and kindergarten of the Institute of Child Welfare at the University of Minnesota; to the children and their teachers of the nursery school, kindergarten, and first and second grades of Northrop Collegiate School in Minneapolis; to the children and their teachers of the nursery school of the New York State College of Home Economics at Cornell University; and to the children and their teachers of the first and second grades of Cayuga Heights School in Ithaca.

The writer is especially grateful to the New York State College of Home Economics at Cornell University for the leave of absence which made the writing of this study possible, and to the members of her department whose willingness to assume her responsibilities made this leave possible. She is also grateful to the staff of the Institute of Child Welfare at the University of Minnesota, and especially to Dr. Florence L. Goodenough for her constructive criticism and encouragement and Dr. John E. Anderson for his helpful suggestions in preparing this manuscript.

CONTENTS

LIST OF TABLES

LIST OF FIGURES

I. INTRODUCTION

For many years attempts have been made to gain an understanding of personality by isolating and analyzing discrete traits such as intelligence, perseverance, introversion-extroversion, emotional stability, and social maturity. Although such analyses have been fruitful in many respects, they fail to give a picture of the total functioning personality. The individual—child or adult—reacts as a whole to each life situation he faces. As the individual grows, his reaction patterns tend to become channelized and he develops his own unique personality. Although it is important to know how intelligent, how emotional, how social an individual is, it is even more important to understand how he combines and uses his specific capacities in responding to a given situation.

Any test that aims to give a comprehensive understanding of the total personality, revealing both intellectual and nonintellectual traits and the functional interaction between the two, merits serious consideration. This is not to say that such a test should be accepted uncritically. The fact that there is a real need for such an instrument does not justify its acceptance without adequate study of the instrument and the claims made for it by its author.

The Rorschach Inkblot Test was developed twenty years ago; since that time it has been used extensively as a clinical aid in revealing personality in both its normal and abnormal aspects. The Rorschach method is a projective technique through which the individual may be encouraged to reveal himself without restraint because he does not know how he is revealing himself and consequently is not inhibited by the norms of his culture. Frank says, "The Rorschach method offers a procedure through which the individual is induced to reveal his 'private world' by telling what he 'sees' in the several cards upon which he may project his meanings, significances, and feelings, just because they are not socially standardized objects or situations to which he must give culturally prescribed responses" (**44**, page 104).

In his description of the Rorschach Test, Piotrowski says:

Thanks to the Rorschach method we can study the living personality in the variety of its aspects much more conveniently by analyzing the reactions to inkblots than through direct observation. I suggest that we look upon these inkblot interpretations as being closely parallel to the subject's intellectual and emotional reactions to his personal environment. Response to inkblots is not a concrete and well defined task as in other attempts of personality measurement where the subject answers logical questions or reacts to a physical stimulus or assumes an attitude toward a practical situation. The flexibility of response to inkblots lies in the multitude of form and color. The subject selects unwittingly those items to which he reacts. These selected areas correspond to those situations of the subject's socio-physical environment to which he has established mental attitudes. Obviously, no one reacts mentally to all stimuli in his environment. The freedom which the subject has in the selection of these areas and in the manner of responding to them assures complete spontaneity in the expression of personality. This is a unique feature of the Rorschach method. To give the subject a definite task to solve or to observe him in a standardized situation is to limit the manifestations of all aspects of his personality. The Rorschach inkblot interpretations should be regarded as a projection of the total personality rather than a specific product of the subject's treatment of an objective situation. They are a direct projection and not an indirect product. The inkblots are a barrier which bar the ordinary environmental stimuli without in any way restraining the subject's individuality. Thus he can freely express his personality insofar as he is in no danger of suffering conflict with reality. The subject does not know what he is revealing of himself during the examination. The inkblots present such a subtle technique that the subject can express himself through them without any effort, and consequently without any restriction of his individuality. (113, pages 23–24.)

In much the same manner as the camera projects a picture of an individual's physical aspects, the Rorschach inkblot technique projects a picture of the individual's personality patterns.

II. REVIEW OF THE LITERATURE

Pre-Rorschach Inkblot Tests

The use of the inkblot technique was first suggested by Binet (21) in 1895.* He noted that different personalities gave different responses to inkblots, the number and form of the responses depending upon the individual giving them. Two years later Dearborn (33) suggested the possibility of using inkblots to study such psychological processes as memory, reaction time, form discrimination, content of consciousness, and imagination. Dearborn (34) studied 16 adult subjects with his 12 sets of 10 inkblots. He found that occupation and habits of living influenced the responses and that age and sex had relatively little effect. Sharp (128) used 10 inkblots with 7 adult subjects and studied the results in terms of number and content of the responses. She reported differences sufficiently marked to permit the classification of her subjects as either constructive and imaginative or matter-of-fact and scientific.

Kirkpatrick (78) seems to have been the first to use inkblots with children. He used 4 inkblots with 500 children in grades 1 to 8. He reported that the younger children gave more responses but were less critical. The older children tended to preface their responses with "it looks like." The younger children were more suggestible, while the older children, as compared with an intermediate group, saw more possibilities. Pyle (118) used 20 inkblots with 151 white school children ranging in age from 8 to 14 years. His findings confirmed those of Kirkpatrick in showing a greater number of associations made by the younger children. The intermediate groups gave fewer, and the older group increased again in number of responses.

Bartlett (3) was the first to introduce color into the inkblot technique. He used 36 blots with 36 subjects of various ages. He anticipated Rorschach in observing that although some subjects responded to the blots as a whole, others responded to details within the blots. Like Rorschach he related the tendency to respond to details to the tendency to give responses that are

* Klopfer and Kelley (87) attribute the first description of inkblots as possible psychological material to Justinus Kerner in 1857. However, it was Binet who first suggested their use as a method of personality diagnosis.

particular and concrete. The tendency to respond to wholes was related to vivid imagination. Some of his subjects reported movement responses. He noted a relationship between responses and the interests and occupations of his subjects. As a result of these observations he divided his subjects into two groups on the basis of "mental action": those who were specific, detailed, and practical and those who were general and imaginative.

Parsons (111) gave the Whipple series 1–10 (153) to 97 subjects aged 7 to 7½ years. Like Rorschach she permitted the subjects to handle and turn the cards and to take unlimited time for their responses. She introduced a practice blot before presenting her test series. She found that 54.4 per cent of the associations given were of animals and human beings. This agrees with Bartlett's findings. Boys gave more war associations (the study was made during wartime) and more landscape associations than did the girls, who gave more animal and human responses. Other sex differences were negligible.

The above studies are not comparable because each investigator used his own series of inkblots and his own techniques of administration. Consequently there is little uniformity in the analysis of responses. The studies are significant, however, because each one emphasizes some useful aspect of the inkblot technique and indicates its possibilities in the study of mental processes.

The Rorschach Inkblot Test

The Rorschach Inkblot Test was developed by Hermann Rorschach, a Swiss psychiatrist, in 1921. He had experimented with the inkblot method for many years before he finally selected, from his series of 60 trial blots, the 10 blots which comprise his test for the diagnosis of personality. He (121) standardized this series on a group of 405 subjects, 117 of whom were normal in mentality and the others abnormal. He classified the responses under four major headings:

1. Mode or manner of apperception: whole or detail
2. Quality of the response: form, movement, or color
3. Content of the response
4. Originality of the response

Each of the classifications was elaborated and identified with specific aspects of personality. The final diagnosis, or picture of personality, depended more upon the sequence of the test factors and the interrelationships between them than upon their frequencies. Rorschach recognized the inadequacy of his norms and the tentativeness of many of his conclusions. He died shortly before the publication of his second contribution, "The Application of the Interpretation of Form to Psychoanalysis" (122).

Post-Rorschach Studies

Interest in the Rorschach Inkblot Test has grown rapidly, as evidenced by the organization of the Rorschach Institute in New York City and the publication of the quarterly, *Rorschach Research Exchange*. While many studies are concerned chiefly with the clinical application of the test and its use as a diagnostic instrument, increasing numbers of investigators are contributing material toward the much needed standardization of procedure, the establishment of norms, and the study of the reliability and validity of the various test determinants.* Since several surveys and bibliographies (Binder, 19; Guirdham, 50; Hertz, 59, 68; Krugman, 90; Piotrowski, 117; and Vernon, 145, 146, 147, 148) are readily available, only those studies which are concerned with the general technique of administration, scoring, and interpretation and with the application of the test to normal children will be included in this review.

General directions for administering the Rorschach Test are given by Rorschach (121) and Rorschach and Oberholzer (122). Considerably more detailed procedures are described by Beck (7), Bochner and Halpern (26), Hertz (57, 59, 62), Klopfer (79, 80, 87), Loosli-Usteri (95), and Vernon (145). Most investigators follow Rorschach's directions and ask, "What could this be?" or "What do you see?" Others (Hertz, 62; Line and Griffin, 94; and Vernon, 145) make some variations in the instructions. Rorschach (121) and Beck (7) advise against the use of any form of instructions that suggests a certain response. Oeser (109) and Kerr (77) disregard this caution in their administration of the test.

Rorschach (121) allowed the subject unlimited time for each inkblot, and this procedure has been followed by later investigators with a few exceptions. Lopfe (97) allowed a maximum of 7 responses for each card. The time allowed for each blot was

* The reader who is unfamiliar with Rorschach terminology is referred to Chapter V of this study and to the Glossary for a description of the various determinants.

limited by Line and Griffin (94) to five minutes and by Hertz (57) to two minutes.

Responses to each blot are recorded verbatim, together with a description of the parts of the blot included in the responses. The efficiency and accuracy of this detailed recording has been improved by the contributions of Beck's symbols (13), Hertz's diagrams (62), Klopfer and Davidson's miniature blot photographs (85), and Vernon's mimeographed blot outlines (145). Hertz (62) and Klopfer and Davidson (85) have published record blanks to facilitate scoring and interpretation.

No essential variation has been made in any aspect of administrative procedure in the use of the Rorschach Test with children. Hertz (57, 62), working with adolescents, recognized that the attitude of the subject to the test unduly influenced his response to the first card. In order to make the first card more comparable with the rest of the series, she introduced a trial blot before starting the test. Kerr (77) found it necessary to simplify Oeser's (109) instructions for use with her group of children, whose ages ranged from 7 to 13 years. Klopfer and Margulies (88) described some of the administrative difficulties involved when the Rorschach Test is given to very young children.

Although the Rorschach Test is relatively simple to administer, it is extremely difficult to score. The variations in terminology among investigators and the lack of concise definition of terms have been clarified to a considerable extent by the publication of manuals by Schneider (126), Loosli-Usteri (96), Rickers-Ovsiankina (119), Beck (13), Bochner and Halpern (26), and Klopfer and Kelley (87). Frequency tabulations have been published by Beck (13) and Hertz (61, 67). The elaboration and refinement of old test determinants (Hertz, 63, 64, 65; Klopfer, 79, 80; Klopfer and Sender, 89; Loosli-Usteri, 96; Monnier, 104, 105; Piotrowski, 114; Thornton, 137; and Vernon, 145) and the addition of new ones (Beck, 8, 11; Hertz, 64; Klopfer, 82; Piotrowski, 114; and Vernon, 146) have improved the objectivity and accuracy of the scoring. The importance of the inquiry in the accurate determination of the test score is emphasized by most of the above investigators. The particular difficulties involved in the inquiry when using the test with very young children is discussed by Klopfer and Margulies (88).

Although the influence of age (Rorschach, 121; Beck, 13;

Behn-Eschenburg, 17; Davidson and Klopfer, 31, 32; Kerr, 77; Loosli-Usteri, 96; Schneider, 126), sex (Behn-Eschenburg, 17; Dubitscher, 36), socio-economic status (Sunne, 135), and race (Lopfe, 97; Loosli-Usteri, 96; Hunter, 72) upon scores has been pointed out by several investigators, only a few studies have been concerned with the establishment of norms for various well-defined groups. Rorschach (121) published norms but he did not describe the groups on which these were based. In addition to his tables, norms have been published for some of the test determinants for normal adults (Dubitscher, 35, 36; Gardner, 48; Guirdham, 50), for mentally retarded adults (Beck, 5, 13), and for superior adults (Beck, 11, 13; Harriman, 53; Hunter, 72; Oeser, 109; Vernon, 145). The most extensive study of norms has been done by Hertz (60, 61, 67), working with adolescents. Norms for various age groups of children from 6 to 16 years old have been published by Behn-Eschenburg (17), Dubitscher (37), Kerr (77), Loosli-Usteri (95, 96), Lopfe (97), Maza (100), and Vernon (145, 146). Some normative data have been reported for highly selected groups of young children by Sunne (135), Paulsen (112), and Klopfer and Margulies (88). Available norms for children will be presented in more detail later in comparison with the findings of the present study.

Relatively few attempts have been made to establish the reliability of the Rorschach Test. The lack of studies in this area is due in part to the difficulty of studying the consistency of the test as a whole. Any attempt to study the reliabilities of the various scoring categories results in only a partial analysis, since the weight of each category in the final synthesis is determined by the relationship between the categories as well as the frequencies within them. Hertz and Rubenstein (70), using the "blind diagnosis" technique, claim reliability for the test as a whole. Troup (140), using a matching technique, found that of six judges three matched all the test-retests correctly, one judge matched 90 per cent, and the other two judges matched 80 per cent. Fosberg (43) found that the test gave consistent results even when the instructions were varied by first asking the subjects to try to make a favorable impression and later asking them to try to make an unfavorable impression. These extreme instructions affected the content of the responses more than any of the test determinants. Fosberg reported correlations in the .90's for standard test-retests and in the .80's for "worst" and "best" tests. He concludes that the test reliabilities are high and that the results cannot be faked. Mira (103) and Wertham and Bleuler (152), using the retest method, found high consistency between first- and second-test results. Neither study presents statistical evidence for the claims made. Kerr (77) found relatively low reliabilities for various test determinants when retests were given a year after the initial tests. Troup (140), giving retests six months after the initial tests, found considerably higher reliabilities for the same test determinants studied by Kerr.

Attempts to study the reliability of the test determinants by means of the split-half method present equally conflicting results. Vernon (145) found low reliabilities for all the test categories studied except the number of responses. On the other hand Hertz (58) reported high reliabilities for practically all the test determinants. Thornton and Guilford (138) found split-half correlations in the .90's for %M and %C and in the .80's for M/C in their Group I. When these same values were calculated for Group II, the coefficients were considerably lower. The available data on reliability will be presented in more detail later. Up to the present time no attempt has been made to study the consistency of the test responses in a group of very young children.

Many attempts have been made to validate the Rorschach Test as a whole. These studies are reviewed in the surveys mentioned previously. In many cases the method employed has been a comparison of the Rorschach diagnoses with available clinical case material. Among investigators claiming high diagnostic validity for the test on the basis of such studies are Beck (4, 6), Behn-Eschenburg (17), Lopfe (97), Mira (103), Oberholzer (108), Rorschach (121), and Schneider (125). The majority of investigators have used the method of contrasted groups to check the validity of the test. Groups contrasted have included all kinds of mental disorders, various intellectual levels, and different age groups (Hertz, 68). Many of the claims made for the Rorschach Test have been substantiated by these studies. A third general method frequently used is that of "blind diagnosis"; that is, the Rorschach record is analyzed by experienced Rorschach testers who are unfamiliar with the subject and know only his sex and approximate age. Hunter (73), Kaplan, Miale, and Clapp (74), Kerr (77), and Troup and

Klopfer (141) claim validity for the test on the basis of this method of analysis. Benjamin and Ebaugh (18) reported 85 per cent complete agreement and 98 per cent agreement in major diagnoses in their comparison of "blind" Rorschach interpretations and clinical findings for a group of 46 mental cases. Vernon (147) matched Rorschach interpretations with personality sketches prepared independently from other data. He found high agreement between the two ($C = +.833$, PE .032).

Because of the interdependence of all factors in the final personality picture, fewer attempts have been made to isolate various categories and to test the specific claims made for each by Rorschach. While results of the clinical studies are in general agreement as to the validity of the instrument, results of attempts to validate the separate categories are conflicting.

Rorschach claimed that his test could differentiate various intellectual levels and in support of his claim presented the relationship between intellectual level and certain of his test categories. This material has been summarized by Beck (7) and is presented in Table 1.

Rorschach's findings have been substantiated in part by Beck (6, 7), Behn-Eschenburg (17), Dubitscher (35), Kerr (77), Schneider (125), and Vernon (145), all of whom employed the method of contrasted groups. The evidence from the few statistical studies is conflicting. Table 2 summarizes the results of three of these studies. Hertz's (57) figures represent the product-moment correlation between the various categories and IQ on the Otis Self-Administering Test, Intermediate Form B. The records of 300 adolescents ranging in age from 12 years 6 months to 16 years 5 months and in IQ from 70 to 139 are included. Hertz combined the five major variables (W, M, %F+, %A, and %O+) into a test battery and obtained a multiple correlation of +.556 with the Otis test scores. Beck's (7) figures are based on a group of 69 feebleminded subjects whose ages ranged from 6 years to 65 years 10 months and whose IQ's on the Stanford-Binet ranged from 21 to 77. His figures in the table represent the product-moment correlation between the various categories and mental age. Vernon's (145) figures represent the product-moment correlation between a composite score on several intelligence tests and the various Rorschach determinants. His group was composed of 25 Yale freshmen ranging in age from 17 to 19 years.

TABLE 1.—RORSCHACH NORMS FOR DIFFERENT INTELLECTUAL LEVELS *

INTELLECTUAL LEVEL	W	M	C	%F+	%A	%O
Very superior	10 or more	over 5	4–7	90–100	10–20	30–50
Superior	7–10	5 or more	1.5–3.5	80–100	20–35	20–30
Average	4–7	2–4	0.5–2.5	70–80	30–55	0–20
Low average	3–4	0–2	1.5–6.0	60–70	50–70	0–20
Morons	1–3	0	4–7	45–60	60–80	30–40
Imbeciles	0–2	0	5.5–8.5	0–45	80–100	40–70

* Table 1 is reprinted from Samuel J. Beck, "The Rorschach Test as Applied to a Feebleminded Group," *Archives of Psychology,* No. 136, p. 38.

TABLE 2.—RELATIONSHIP BETWEEN VARIOUS TEST FACTORS AND INTELLIGENCE

TEST FACTOR	HERTZ		BECK		VERNON	
	COEFFICIENT	PE	COEFFICIENT	PE	COEFFICIENT	PE *
W	+.241	.038	+.474	.06	+.09	...
%W					+.23	...
M	+.259	.038	+.256	.079	−.05	...
%M					+.10	...
C-score	+.209	.038	+.012	.080 †	+.25	...
%F+	+.460	.032	+.640	.051	+.09	...
%A	−.108	.038	+.156	.079	+.26	...
%P					+.12	...
%O			−.391	.070	−.11	...
%O+	+.398	.032				

* *PE* was not reported.
† Mean C response.

It should be noted that the investigators cited in Table 2 worked with relatively homogeneous groups, and consequently the correlations found would be expected to be lower than if a wider range of intellectual abilities had been correlated with the various test factors. However, evidence from these studies indicates a low correlation between intelligence and each of the variables, with the possible exception of %F+. On the other hand, Kerr (77) reports a product-moment correlation of +.57 between IQ and W, −.14 between IQ and %A, and −.29 between W and %A. On the basis of her findings Kerr concludes that Rorschach's claims hold but that the only significant relationship is the one between IQ and W.

A few attempts have been made to study the validity of various nonintellectual determinants. Rorschach claimed that color scores give a measure of the subject's emotionality. Hertz (57) reported a tetrachoric correlation of +.66 between stable and unstable groups classified on the basis of the Woodworth-Mathews total scores. She concluded that color scores tend to indicate neurotic tendencies and hence the degree of emotional balance. Statistically reliable differences were found for M, %A, %O, and P scores between the stable and unstable groups. Her findings do not agree with those of Line and Griffin (94), who also contrasted stable and unstable groups. Beck (7) reported a zero relationship between affectivity and mental age.

Beck (7) supported Rorschach's claim that P is an index of adaptability, or the ability to conform with social groups. He contrasted a socially cooperative group with the rest of his experimental group and reported a higher P score for the members of the cooperative group.

Rorschach's claim that DS is a measure of negativism or obstinacy has been questioned by the studies of Lopfe (97), Beck (7), and Vernon (145). However, Hertz (57) found a significant difference in DS between normal and maladjusted groups.

It was Rorschach's claim that the ratio of M (inner creativity or power of introversion) to C-score (affectivity or power of extroversion) represented a measure of the experience type (*Erlebnistyp*). Enke (41) and Levy and Beck (91) supported this claim by studies indicating a relationship between manic tendencies and extroversion, and between depressive tendencies and introversion. Vernon (145) found no relationship between Rorschach's M : C ratio and a composite score based on the Neymann-Kohlstadt questionnaire of introversion-extroversion and various other measures of sociality. Thornton and Guilford (138) correlated Rorschach scores (M, %M, C, and log M/C) with scores on the Nebraska Personality Inventory. They concluded that Rorschach *Erlebnistyp* scores, as determined in their experiment, showed little or no relation to those factors of introversion-extroversion measured by the Nebraska Inventory. Paulsen (112) reported that a large majority of her 6-year-olds showed an extroversal M : C-sum relationship. Beck (7) found that his feebleminded group showed a reliable tendency to be impulsive and extroverted rather than creative and introverted. Since this result agrees with what is already known of the feebleminded, he concludes that the M : C-sum is valid as claimed by Rorschach.

Hertz (57) correlated Rorschach introversive-extroversive scores with scores made on the Brush Modification of the Allport Ascendency-Submission Test. She reported a tetrachoric correlation of +.86 for her group (164 cases). This supports Rorschach's claim that a predominance of color responses indicates ascendant qualities, while a predominance of motion responses indicates submissive qualities. Hertz reported statistically reliable differences for M, C, %A, %O, and P between the ascendant and submissive groups. Klopfer (82) suggests the use of R(VIII–X) : Total R as a more reliable measure of introversion-extroversion than the commonly used M : C-score. If the ratio exceeds 40 per cent the subject is more affected by stimuli from without. If the ratio is under 30 per cent the subject responds little or not at all to stimuli from without. This claim is as yet unverified.

III. THE PROBLEM

The present problem grew out of the writer's interest in the research on the Rorschach Test which was being done by Hertz (57) at the Brush Foundation. Since the test gave promise of being a valuable instrument in the study of adolescents, the question naturally arose, "Can the Rorschach Test be applied at the preschool level?" No answer was available in 1936 when the present study was undertaken. At that time the writer made a preliminary study of a group of 20 preschool children ranging in age from 24 to 48 months to determine how early in life the Rorschach Test could be given. The writer was interested also in any clues which might suggest modifications and clarification of administrative procedures. The results were encouraging with children of 3 years and over. They were interested in the test, and their responses were of varied length and content. Children under 3 years showed little interest in the test, and considerable urging was necessary to keep them at the task. Incomplete records often resulted.

Since 1936 the Rorschach Test has been used increasingly with preschool children. Several institutions (Vassar, Wheaton, Sarah Lawrence, Visitation Academy, Temple, and Harvard) are using the Rorschach Test with preschool children. Preschool Rorschach records from these institutions (205 records of 155 children between 2 and 7 years of age) have been analyzed by Klopfer and Margulies (88), but up to the present time no attempt has been made to check the reliability of the test or to validate any of the test determinants at the preschool level. Nor is there any detailed publication of the results of Rorschach records of preschool children.

The present study has four major aims:

1. To refine administrative procedures and to simplify instructions so that they are meaningful to young children.
2. To study variations in test determinants along with variations in chronological age, mental age, and sex and to present these findings as a tentative basis for future standardization of the test in its application to young children.
3. To study the reliability of the various test determinants at the preschool level.

4. To check the validity of certain specific claims made by Rorschach as to the meaning of the various test determinants.

This investigation does not attempt to validate or invalidate the Rorschach Test as a clinical instrument, nor is it meant to be an exhaustive analysis of the test in all its controversial aspects. Such a problem is beyond the scope of a single investigation. Its purpose is the application of the Rorschach Test to a selected group of young children and the analysis of results in terms of age, sex, mental ability, and various measurable aspects of personality. It is essentially an exploratory study and as such should raise more problems than it attempts to solve.

IV. PROCEDURE

Description of the Test

The Rorschach Test consists of a standard series of 10 bilaterally symmetrical inkblot designs. These blots vary in size between 5 and 7¾ inches on the horizontal axis and between 3½ and 6¼ inches on the vertical axis. Each blot is centered on a stiff, white card 7 by 9½ inches. In 5 of the blots (I, IV, V, VI, and VII) only black ink is used; in 2 blots (II and III) red and black inks are used; and in 3 blots (VIII, IX, and X) several colored inks are used. The cards are numbered and are always presented in the same order.

The technique of administering the test is essentially the same as that for any other individual test. The subject is seated comfortably and good rapport is established before the test begins. With adult subjects the examiner usually introduces the test by a general description of how inkblots are made. Some examiners demonstrate the making of inkblots; some use a trial blot for explanatory purposes; others omit both the demonstration and the trial blot and proceed as quickly as possible with the presentation of the test. The subject is asked to tell what he sees. Although there is no standardized wording for these introductory remarks, there is a general agreement among Rorschach workers that they should be noncommittal and so phrased as to secure maximum cooperation by relieving any embarrassment, apprehension, or tension. A relaxed, easy atmosphere is essential for the test. It is also necessary that the subject be made to feel that there are no right answers and that all responses are equally acceptable.

The cards are presented to the subject one at a time. Each card is handed to the subject in an upright position, but he is free to turn it as he wishes, although he is not told that he may do so. No time limit is set. When the subject feels that he has finished responding to a card he may indicate this by placing the card face down on the table. The subject's verbatim responses and the time between the presentation of the card and the first response are recorded. A record is also kept of questions, remarks, exclamations, and emotional expressions such as giggling and laughing.

After the series has been completed once, it is customary to go through it a second time. This second presentation is called the inquiry. Its purposes are twofold: to help the examiner in his subsequent scoring and interpretation by permitting him to secure more definite information as to the location of the responses and their determinants, and to permit the subject to supplement spontaneously his previous remarks.

Administration of the Test to Young Children

The administration of the Rorschach Test to young children is complicated by the difficulties inherent in any testing of young children, who, especially at the preschool age, are easily distracted and are apt to tire of any task that requires sustained attention to one type of material. They are extremely sensitive to the adult working with them, and if she is a stranger rapport may be difficult to establish. Furthermore, young children are less inhibited than adults in revealing themselves through subtle psychomotor tensions, gestures, and more or less systematized forms of communications which are quite intelligible to those close to them but which may leave a stranger baffled and uncertain of their meanings. Any verbal test used with young children must reckon with a language hazard. Particularly is this true in the Rorschach Test, where the record depends upon the ability to verbalize.

On the other hand, there are distinct advantages in working with young children in a testing situation. If the child knows the adult and accepts her, and if the adult knows children and feels free in her contacts with them, rapport is easily established. The young child's life experience is less structuralized and less inhibited than that of an adult. He has had fewer conflicts with cultural norms and consequently feels less compelled to conform to a prescribed mode of behavior. In rapport with an adult the child expresses himself freely and revealingly. Especially is this true when he is alone with an accepted adult in a simple situation where he is not outwardly challenged to competition.

Fully aware of the advantages and difficulties that are involved in testing young children, the writer attempted to set up the present study in such a manner as to capitalize on the advantages and minimize the difficulties.

THE TESTING SETUP

All tests were given in the school buildings in a room as free from distractions as possible. The child was seated, with his back to the windows, on a small chair at a small table. In no case was artificial lighting necessary. The examiner sat beside and slightly behind the child so that he could see her if he wished and yet not be unduly distracted by her presence. In each case the child and the examiner were alone in the room. All children were familiar with the testing room, and all had had at least one previous experience in an adult-child testing situation since all children had taken at least one mental test.

EMOTIONAL PREPARATION

All Rorschach records were taken during the morning shortly after the child's arrival at school, so that the fatigue and hunger factors were minimized. The younger children were taken to the toilet before the test. All the subjects in this study had many contacts with the writer during the normal school day. The writer was known to the preschool children as a member of the preschool staff and as a daily participant in their activities. The first- and second-grade children had fewer contacts with the examiner but all knew her. Contacts with the older children before the Rorschach Test consisted of cooperation on one or two mental tests, participation in playground games, and, in the case of the Northrop children, daily contact at lunch.*

This opportunity for mutual familiarity between adult and child is an extremely important factor in emotional preparation for any testing situation. A child who feels at ease and secure with an adult comes willingly from the group—often begging for the opportunity. He has a positive mental set of anticipated pleasure and with minimum preparation is ready to begin a test. Because young children tire easily, it is important to get a test under way quickly. If much valuable time has to be consumed in the establishment of rapport, the test results suffer. The writer is inclined to minimize the objection that an adult familiar with a particular child is at a disadvantage with that child in the testing situation. Any adult trained in psychological and psychometric principles should be so constantly aware of the goal of the specific test she is using that she temporarily subor-

* For a description of the subject groups see page 30.

dinates, during the testing session, any personal bias she may have.

PRESENTATION OF THE TEST

In general the administrative technique described by Rorschach (121, 122) was followed, but the age of the subjects made certain modifications necessary. The cards were presented in an upright position and the child was not permitted to rotate them. This modification was forced by grim necessity rather than by meditative logic. During preliminary experimentation it was apparent that preschool children occupied themselves primarily with the actual manipulation of the card rather than with the changing configuration of the inkblot. An attempt was made to devise a simple apparatus for the successive presentation of the cards. This apparatus was soon abandoned because it lengthened the presentation time and added to the formality of the test when informality was one of the principles necessary to obtain free responses. Instead, the child was handed the card and when he first attempted to turn it, he was told, "You hold it this way." If further attempts at rotation occurred the instructions were repeated. The older child often made no attempt to turn the card.

A second modification which seemed desirable was the introduction of a trial inkblot preceding the test. Hertz (57, 62) initiated this procedure when she found that test scores were influenced by the subject's initial attitude toward the test. Her purposes in introducing a homemade trial blot were to make the first card more comparable with the following ones and to establish a favorable mental set at the beginning of the test (62). With young children the trial blot served the further purpose of nonverbal orientation in the type of material which was to follow. The homemade trial inkblot, like the Rorschach cards, was bilaterally symmetrical and was made with black ink on white paper. An outline of the blot appears in Figure 1. The same blot was used with all subjects.

After considerable preliminary experimentation, simplified instructions were adopted. Because young children are easily confused by detailed descriptions, the directions were made as brief as possible. When the child was seated comfortably the examiner said, "I have something to show you." The trial blot was then presented and the examiner continued, "What could this be?" If the subject hesitated more than ten seconds the examiner said, "Tell me all about it. What could this be?" With normal children of 3 years and over, these instructions should be sufficient if adequate rapport has been established. No child in the present study needed further directions or more initial encouragement. If the child stopped after one re-

Figure 1.—OUTLINE OF THE TRIAL BLOT

sponse the examiner said, "Yes? Can you tell me more?" These directions were used with each blot in the series. Throughout the test the examiner expressed interest and encouragement. Questions were answered naturally but briefly, and care was taken to avoid any suggestion which would influence the test responses. When the child indicated that he was finished with the trial blot the examiner asked, "Is that all? When you finish, give it to me and I will give you a new one." No time limit was set. The child was free to give up the blot after one response or to continue to give as many responses as he wished.

After the child had completed the series once, the cards were presented a second time and he was asked to locate his previous responses. Generally the simple question "Where is the ......?" was sufficient to get the necessary explanation. With the younger children the inquiry was almost unnecessary, since they usually accompanied their first responses with descriptive gestures such as pointing to or tracing with their fingers the parts of the blot included in their interpretation. This was fortunate, for the younger children were apt to become impatient with the inquiry and to lose interest in the material. "I told you that one," "All done now," and "Can I go out now?" were frequent responses to the inquiry, and very few spontaneous remarks were added. Older children were less impatient, but many of them showed a decided loss of interest. They were cooperative, however, when the examiner explained, "I want to see just what you saw. Perhaps you can help me." Every attempt was made to have the inquiry as brief as possible.

RECORDING RESPONSES

Before starting the test the examiner had readily available the trial blot, the Rorschach cards, a stop watch, pencils, forms for recording verbatim responses, and tracings of the blots with parts numbered for easy identification. The trial blot and the Rorschach cards are described above. The stop watch was quiet enough to be inaudible to the child, who was unaware that any timing was being done. A simple mimeographed form was used for recording responses. Space was provided at the top for the name, address, father's occupation, CA, IQ, date of the test, and date of birth. The remainder of the sheet was divided into four columns for recording reaction time, verbatim responses, inquiry information, and scoring. This form was quite similar to the one reported by Hertz (62). Tracings of the 10 blots were numbered according to the symbols used by Beck (13). When the various parts of the blot were used in the responses, it was possible to record them by a simple numerical symbol and thus to reduce the time for recording without loss to subsequent scoring.

V. SCORING AND INTERPRETATION

Responses to the Rorschach inkblots are scored in four principal categories: the manner of apperception, the quality of the response, the content of the response, and the degree of originality. The original German symbols have been translated into English equivalents and are in general use among Rorschach workers in this country. Two Rorschach manuals (26, 87) are now available. Although both contribute to ease and accuracy of administration, scoring, and interpretation, neither makes essential variations in the scoring used by previous writers. Neither had been published when the records in the present study were scored.

In scoring the records the writer followed Rorschach's original instructions (121) supplemented by the work of Beck (13), Hertz (61), and Rickers (119). Since Rorschach, Beck, and Rickers were concerned primarily with normal and abnormal adult records and Hertz with adolescent records, the writer hesitated to adopt many of the details of their scoring procedures. For example, could it be assumed because a detail in a figure was rarely responded to by adults, that a response to this same detail by young children would constitute a rare-detail answer? Is an adult poor-form response a legitimate criterion for marking the same response poor form when given by a young child? Are original and popular responses identical for adults and children? Or is it not possible that certain popular adult responses might constitute original responses when given by young children whose life experiences are necessarily limited? These and countless other problems of scoring were in mind throughout the project. Since all previous workers with children had used adult norms and since no norms were available for young children, the writer saw no alternative to this very questionable procedure of using adult norms. Drawing what support and comfort she could from the statement of Klopfer and Margulies (88) that basically the same interpretative principles could be applied to Rorschach reactions in early childhood as in adulthood, the writer continued the practice of her predecessors in the matter of scoring. A brief description of the symbols used and a suggestion of their implications in interpretation follows.*

Symbols Used to Describe the Manner of Apperception

W—response to the figure as a whole. The subject responds to the entire blot but does not include the white spaces in and around the blot. Rorschach says that the scoring of W responses is self-evident. This statement is misleading since there are at least two major types of W responses, signifying very different mental processes. In the first type, usually called primary or structural, the subject responds to the crude form of the blot. Little or no organization or abstraction takes place. In the second type, the combinatory, the subject first breaks up or analyzes the component parts of the blot and then reorganizes and relates these parts into a W response. For obvious reasons the distinction between the two types of W responses is extremely difficult and, in the case of very young children, almost impossible. Rorschach claimed that a high number of W responses represents an emphasis on abstract forms of thinking and indicates the utilization of logical and constructive mental capacities.

DW—response to the figure as a whole. It differs from the simple W response because in this case the subject responds to one detail and, overlooking other details, gives a response to the blot as a whole. In normal records responses of this sort are said to indicate a tendency to impulsive and intuitive thinking and to indicate imagination rather than objectivity.

WS—response to the figure as a whole, including the adjacent white spaces. Very little significance has been attached to S when it appears in combination with a W response.

D—response to frequently selected details of the figure. Rorschach (121) said that D responses can be defined statistically but that this procedure is unnecessary because, after giving the test to 50 normals, one knows most of the normal details. Both Beck (13) and Rickers (119) have published lists of normal and rare-detail responses based on their experience with the test. Hertz (57) is the first and, up to the present time, the only investigator to attempt the statistical determination of detail and rare-detail responses. She designated all responses to details

* See also the Glossary, pp. 101–4.

which, in her group, were above the twentieth percentile in frequency as D responses, and all those below the twentieth percentile as Dr responses. In the present study reference to each of the above sources was made before scoring D responses. Whenever there was disagreement among these sources, Hertz's tables were followed. Rorschach claimed that a tendency to give D responses is associated with a concrete, practical approach to problems.

Dr—response to rarely selected details of the figure. The procedure for scoring Dr responses was identical with that outlined above for D responses. Rorschach claimed that the tendency to give Dr responses may indicate the keen observer. In some cases Dr responses indicate normal emphasis on and concern for detail, whereas in other cases these responses indicate overprecision and maladjustment.

Do—oligophrenic detail. The subject interprets only part of a human or animal when most people see the whole body clearly. Do responses occur primarily in the records of feebleminded subjects.

DS—response to the white spaces within or adjacent to the blot. In normal subjects this response occurs very infrequently and is usually classified as a rare-detail response. Rorschach claimed that S responses are always indicative of some sort of tendency to opposition, the direction of opposition depending upon the relationship of S to the other determinants.

Symbols Used to Describe the Quality of the Response

F—response in which form is the sole determinant of the interpretation. Most responses are determined by the form or shape of the blot. F responses may be good or poor depending on how frequently they are given, whether or not they are easily apparent to others, and whether or not they are clearly perceived by the subject. Good F responses are scored F+ and poor F responses are scored F−. Rorschach claimed that statistical methods were used for the determination of good and poor forms, but he gave no explanation of his method other than the statement that form answers given by 100 subjects were used as the norm. From these a definite range of normal and frequently occurring form visualization could be defined. These responses were called "good forms" (F+). Thus many forms which would not have been called good on the basis of subjective evaluation alone were designated F+. Responses better than these were also called F+ and those which were less clear F—. Rorschach believed that although subjective judgment was still necessary in determining F+ and F—, this evaluation could be made with relative certainty (121, page 23).

Although Beck (13) and Rickers (119) were referred to for the scoring of the F category in the present study, Hertz (57) was again accepted as the final authority in the determination of F+ and F—. Hertz bases her scoring of F+ and F— responses on three conditions: All frequencies which, in her group, fell above the fiftieth percentile were considered good form; all F responses which received a low frequency but which belonged to a similar group or class were scored as that group was scored; all forms were scored according to the concurrent estimate of three to five judges.

Rorschach maintained that a high percentage of F+ indicates the ability to concentrate, the possession of sharply formed memory images, the ability to recall these memory images into consciousness, and the ability to select the most suitable of the various images which arise. Thus %F+ is an indicator of intelligence.

M—response indicating an experience of felt movement. Since M responses are *ipso facto* F responses, movement always being movement of forms, all M responses are either M+ or M— according to whether the form element is F+ or F—. Some recent investigators (26) distinguish between human and animal movement responses. Human forms seen in action are usually scored M, animal forms in action are scored FM, and inanimate objects reported in action are scored m. Rorschach did not make this distinction. He claimed that only when human beings or animals capable of motion similar to that of human beings (monkeys, bears) are seen in the figures can the responses be considered as kinesthetically determined (121, page 25).

Since the prime requisite of a response is that the subject feel the actual sensation of motion, and since young children seem to identify themselves with animals as freely as with human beings, no distinction was made in the scoring of this category in the present study.

Rorschach believed that M responses represent a component of intelligence which parallels the freedom of association and the number of individual (original) responses. Consequently M is closely allied with the emotional processes. It is indicative of emotional energy (more unconscious than conscious) and of the energy of associative activity inherent in the disposition of the individual subject. This component of intelligence represents the ability to create new, individual productions, the capacity for "inner creation." (121, page 65.)

C—response in which color is the sole determinant of the response. Rorschach claimed that subjects who are stable emotionally give few or no color answers (121, page 31). Pure C responses, therefore, are indicative of uncontrolled emotional responses to the environment, i.e., impulsiveness.

CF—response in which color constitutes the primary and form the secondary determinant of the response. Rorschach said that CF answers occur more frequently than C responses. CF responses always appear where C answers are given, but the inverse of this does not hold. CF answers are frequently given by normals whereas C answers are not. CF responses are more frequently given by women than by men. They are indicative of emotional instability, irritability, sensitivity, and suggestibility. (121, page 33.)

FC—response in which form constitutes the primary and color the secondary determinant of the response. Rorschach claimed that FC responses are indicative of "that emotional instability biologically necessary and basic for the ability to achieve emotional rapport and to make emotional approach to the environment." C and CF responses indicate the more "egocentric affective responsiveness," and FC responses indicate "the more adaptive effective responsiveness." No C, CF, or FC responses occur in the records of completely stabilized subjects, the depressed, the indolent, and the pedantic. (121, page 33.)

Cn—response in which color is named with no attempt at interpretation. Color naming is said to occur only in the records of abnormal subjects or normal subjects responding while in an abnormal state.

K—chiaroscuro response. These responses are determined at least in part by the various shading values of the blot. Many subdivisions of this test factor have been suggested by recent investigators, and considerable confusion exists concerning symbolic scoring and interpretation. Bochner and Halpern (26) divide chiaroscuro responses into two major groups: Those which involve vista and perspective in their interpretation are scored K, and those which are determined by the effect of texture and surface quality are scored c. They believe that K responses indicate a basic instability. "Repeated occurrence of such responses implies that the individual's general outlook is a melancholy one, that he has a tendency to react to depressive feelings of anxiety. These feelings may best be described by the term 'free floating anxiety.' The person is generally anxious, but his disturbance is not localized, and he does not know what is troubling him. When form becomes a concomitant of the K response, that is, when the response is scored KF and FK, the cause of the anxiety becomes more specific, showing at least some awareness on the part of the individual of what is disturbing him. The FK response with the intellectual factor dominant reveals a self-critical awareness which, in an individual with introversive capacity, implies the ability to introspect. K responses of all kinds indicate feelings of insecurity and wishful thinking. . . . The individual giving several c responses will be sensitive and sympathetic, the direction of that sensitivity depending upon whether he is predominantly outgoing or primarily self-absorbed. In the extratensive person the c response will mean tact and sympathy. Found in this setting it adds nuance and tenderness to an otherwise forthright emotionality. In the introverted person it means shyness, anxiety, and caution, which may make his adjustment a painful one. When form is not a part of the c answer we have sensuality." (26, pages 50–51.)

Symbols Used to Describe the Content of the Response

A—animal. The blot or some part of it is interpreted as a whole animal. If, however, the interpretation does not include the whole animal but refers merely to some part of an animal, the scoring is Ad (animal detail). From the point of view of frequency the A response ranks first. Rorschach claimed that all intelligent subjects give from 25 per cent to 50 per cent A responses. Imaginative subjects tend to give fewer. Thus a high percentage of A responses indicates stereotypy.

H—human response. The blot or some part of it is interpreted as a complete human form. If the interpretation refers merely to some part of the human form the response is scored Hd (human detail). According to Rorschach, most normally intelligent individuals interpret more whole human forms than detail human forms, whereas unintelligent individuals give more Hd responses than H responses.

Few special significances have been ascribed to any of the other content categories. Some investigators maintain that range of interest is indicated by the number of categories represented in an individual record.

Symbols Used to Describe the Degree of Originality

O—original response. An original response is universally defined as an answer that occurs but once in 100 tests. O responses are generally divided into two groups, good original responses (O+) and poor original responses (O−), depending upon the quality of the F responses with which they are associated.

At present the scoring of O responses is highly subjective and depends upon the experience of the scorer. Since there is no theoretical limit to the number of possible original answers, it is almost impossible to set up objective criteria for the scoring of this category. In scoring the records in the present study, the writer referred constantly to the sample records of Rorschach (121), Beck (13), Rickers (119), and Hertz (57). O responses indicate an ability to depart from the commonplace and a capacity for perceiving new relationships.

P—popular response. A popular response is defined by Rorschach as an answer given one in three times in response to a blot or part of a blot. Later investigators have generally accepted one in six times as the criterion for the determination of the popular response. The latter definition has been used in scoring the records in the present study, and constant reference has been made to P responses as listed by Beck (13), Rickers (119), and Hertz (57).

According to Bochner and Halpern, "The giving of a popular answer indicates an ability to think in line with the group, to share in the thoughts of one's fellow men. It implies an intellectual and emotional adaptation to the life about one, a participation in the 'herd' reaction. It shows a receptivity to public opinion and a desire to conform. The number of popular answers any subject will give is dependent upon several factors, these being primarily his intelligence, his emotional stability, and his age." (26, page 65.)

Other Symbols Used in the Test

R—the total number of responses to the series of ten ink-blots. R is dependent upon both intellectual and emotional factors and is significant only in relation to the quality of the responses and to the other test determinants. Bochner and Halpern state that a large number of responses are given by "(1) the intelligent who are rich in ideas, who have no difficulty in expressing themselves, and who are not inhibited because of emotional disturbances, (2) the unintelligent who think this is a very easy task compared with others that are given them. These people have no insight into their limitations and so are not disturbed or inhibited by their lack. . . . (3) There are also the highly imaginative, artistic individuals whose records are rich and show a considerable number of original responses, (4) the ambitious who show their ability quantitatively, (5) thorough individuals who cover a plate systematically using every available stimulus, and (6) those who are in good humor and a happy frame of mind, who wish to oblige and because of their emotional state can do so without effort. Few responses are given by (1) the intelligent who are highly critical of everything they produce, and so limit their output to what they consider the one or two best possible answers to each blot, (2) the unintelligent who have some insight into their limitations and so exercise some censorship over their productions. Because they know they are not bright, they are afraid that what they do is wrong and they are ashamed. (3) The ambitious who show their ability qualitatively, (4) the depressed and others who are emotionally inhibited, (5) the indifferent, the unobliging, and the ill-humored as well as those with whom good rapport has not been established, (6) various forms of the mentally diseased." (26, pages 70–71.)

Obj—the total number of persons or objects mentioned in response to the series. This is essentially a simple noun count and as far as can be determined is comparable to Hertz's "items."

OL—organizational links. This represents the number of logical connections within a record. For example, the response "a man walking on a fence" would receive the store 2 OL. Since this category is introduced here for the first time, its possible significance will be indicated in the results of this study.

Relationship between Symbols

It should be emphasized that claims for the diagnostic significance of the above symbols depend primarily on their interrelation within an individual record. For the sake of brevity and because these interrelations are discussed in detail elsewhere (26, 87, 121, and in the publications of the Rorschach Institute), many important interpretative meanings have been omitted. One of these relationships is so universally referred to that it seems wise to mention it briefly. M : C-sum refers to the ratio of the total number of M responses to the color-sum. This latter value is calculated by assigning an arbitrary numerical value of 0.5 to FC responses, 1.0 to CF responses, and 1.5 to C responses. The ratio of M : C is claimed to indicate how the individual experiences (*Erlebnistyp*). Since M responses indicate inner creativity and C responses indicate outward response to the environment, the ratio between the two is said to indicate introversive and extratensive trends. This and other relationships between determinants will be discussed in greater detail later in this study.

Records in this study were scored as soon as possible after they were taken. The scores were recorded on raw-data sheets according to the accepted convention. That is, the first symbol represented the manner of apperception, the second group of symbols the quality of the response, and the third symbol the content of the response. The occurrence of O or P responses was noted after the other symbols. After the scoring was completed the symbols were recorded on a summary sheet.

VI. THE SUBJECTS

The distribution according to age and sex of the 123 subjects in this study is indicated in Table 3. The subjects ranged in age between 3 and 8 years and there were approximately as many boys as girls. At the time of their tests the 77 preschool children were enrolled in one of the following groups: the University of Minnesota nursery school or kindergarten, Northrup Collegiate nursery school or kindergarten, or the nursery school of the New York State College of Home Economics at Cornell University. The 46 older children were drawn from the first and second grades of either Northrup Collegiate School in Minneapolis or Cayuga Heights School in Ithaca.

Fifty-five of the preschool children were given retests approximately one month after the initial tests. Stanford-Binet (Form L) records were available for each of the 123 children. The mental tests had been given one to four months before the Rorschach Test except in the case of the Cayuga Heights children, who were given their mental tests the day before they took the Rorschach. In addition to the mental test record, teachers' ratings of each subject were secured on the Olson Behavior Rating Scale (Schedule B). Since this schedule was devised for children above preschool age, certain items not well adapted to the early ages were omitted. Teachers' ratings for 30 of the preschool children were secured on the Marston Introversion-Extroversion Rating Scale.

The subjects in this study constitute a highly homogeneous group both in intelligence and in socio-economic status. The range in IQ was from 90 to 157 with an average of 124.35

TABLE 3.—DISTRIBUTION OF SUBJECTS ACCORDING TO AGE AND SEX

AGE	NUMBER OF CASES		
	BOYS	GIRLS	BOTH
3-0 to 3-11	13	12	25
4-0 to 4-11	12	15	27
5-0 to 5-11	11	14	25
6-0 to 6-11	11	12	23
7-0 to 7-11	10	13	23
Total	57	66	123

(*SD* 14.20). All the children came from homes where the fathers were in socio-economic groups I, II, or III of the Minnesota Occupational Scale. The majority (67.4 per cent) had fathers who were in one of the professions; 22.0 per cent had fathers who were business executives; and 10.6 per cent had fathers who were in one of the various classifications of group III. All came from relatively small families. Over a fourth (29.3 per cent) were only children, 48.0 per cent had one sibling, 15.4 per cent had two, 4.9 per cent had three, and 2.4 per cent had four.

VII. THE USE OF THE RORSCHACH TEST WITH YOUNG CHILDREN

Three major problems are involved in the study of any test. Does the test measure what it claims to measure? How consistent are these measurements? These are the familiar questions of validity and reliability. In addition there is a third question: Under what conditions may the test be expected to achieve maximum efficiency of measurement? The purpose of this study is to seek answers to the above questions in respect to the use of the Rorschach Test with young children. The problems of reliability and validity will be discussed later. The question of conditions for the maximum efficiency of the Rorschach Test with young children is the concern of the present chapter.

Perhaps the most important condition contributing to the maximum efficiency of a test—especially of any test used with young children—is the nature of the test material. Unless this material is interesting and appealing in itself, attempts to safeguard its administration are almost futile. The subject may be led to the material and the best of rapport may be established, but it is the young child's initial contact with the material that determines to a large extent whether or not he will have any further dealings with the matter. Only when the test material is acceptable to the child can the child and adult pull together toward a mutual goal.

On the basis of experience in this study the Rorschach material seems to fulfill the condition of inherent interest. The subjects accepted the inkblots and were willing to verbalize their meanings. Some difficulty was involved in the lack of variety in the test. Sustained attention is difficult for young children and for this reason tests with varied content are more interesting to them. Then too, many young children, for various reasons, prefer nonverbal to verbal test situations, and a test which alternates verbal and nonverbal items has a distinct advantage over a purely verbal test. After six or seven of the Rorschach cards had been interpreted, some children showed signs of satiation with the material, but with encouragement all were willing to complete the series. Although the Rorschach does not have as much inherent interest for the preschool child as the Merrill-Palmer or the new Stanford-Binet, nevertheless the ink-blot material has sufficient appeal to make it acceptable to the preschool child.

A second condition essential for the maximum efficiency of a test is that its goal must be clearly defined and accepted by both the examiner and the subject. The administrative goal of the Rorschach Test is simply to secure a verbal expression of what the subject sees in the inkblots. As has been pointed out previously, it is often easier for the child than for the adult to express freely what he sees, since the child is unaware that he is revealing himself by his expression. Whereas the accurate record of an adult may be difficult to obtain because of his inhibitions, the record of a very young child is more apt to be influenced by his lack of ability to maintain the set of the test. When a child loses a set goal, he seeks whatever diversion presents itself or else he creates his own. These self-created diversions are well known to every worker with young children. They have to be met as they occur according to the skill and experience of the worker. It is important, however, to reduce to a minimum any diversion which can be foreseen.

Early in the preliminary experimentation it was evident that the young child was unduly concerned with the manipulation of the Rorschach card. He felt it, patted it, smelled it, and sometimes kissed it. Occasionally he pushed it off the table or threw it on the floor. More often he became engrossed in the manipulative possibilities. Not only did he inspect the card from all angles, but he was equally concerned with examining the back of the card. In fact, his interest in manipulation became primary and only secondarily, if at all, was he concerned with meanings. It became necessary to safeguard the goal of the test by reducing the possibilities for manipulation. Even the youngest children accepted the decision to limit the way the card was held to the upright position. With this change in procedure a marked increase in attention to the blot was noted.

The effect of this major variation of procedure on the Rorschach records cannot be determined from this study since the stationary position was used throughout. It is possible that the total number of responses might be reduced. On the other hand, improved attention to the upright position might so increase the number of interpretations in this position as to compensate at least in part for the lack of opportunity to interpret the blot at other angles. Some implications can be drawn concerning the effect of this change in procedure when the Rorschach records in this study are compared with those of other investigators in Chapter VIII.

A third condition contributing to the maximum efficiency of any test is the development of clear, concise directions. In the case of young children it is important that these directions be simple and brief. Whenever possible, demonstration rather than lengthy verbal instructions is desirable. For this reason the introduction of a trial blot is especially important when using the Rorschach Test with young children. This procedure is more effective than any verbal attempt to explain the nature of the task. Rorschach's question, "What could this be?" is simple and brief and was easily understood by the young children in this study.

Since much of the Rorschach literature stresses the need for flexibility in the administration of the test, and since this emphasis has often been used as an excuse for loose administrative procedures, it seems desirable to stress here that flexibility and standardization of procedure are not diametrically opposed. Any test benefits by the standardization of procedure. When a standardized procedure has been adopted, it may be used either rigidly or flexibly. The parrotlike mouthing of a set of rote directions is rigid to the point of being meaningless. The speaking of these identical directions in a person-to-person relationship in a total situation allows all the flexibility implied in the cooperation of two unique personalities momentarily directed toward a common task. Rigidity and flexibility are qualities inherent in people and are reflected in their utilization of materials. It is just as possible to have rigidity in nonstandardized procedures as in standardized procedures and, conversely, it is equally possible to have flexibility in standardized and nonstandardized procedures.

A fourth condition contributing to the efficiency of any test is a clearly defined basis for the continued encouragement of the subject. Too much concern is generally expressed for the form of this encouragement and too little emphasis placed on its purpose, which is to create a feeling of security, adequacy, and general well-being. Encouragement should be used judiciously throughout the Rorschach to further rapport and to keep the child's attention focused on the test. Since there is wide variation in both kind and amount of encouragement required by individual children, standardization is impossible. With the young child especially, expressions of encouragement should be neither wordy nor profuse. Often the most effective form is nonverbal. A timely smile or pat, an appreciative chuckle with the child, a relaxed, calm attitude of acceptance and anticipation are more meaningful and far less distracting than many verbal comments.

The major difficulty encountered in the use of the Rorschach Test with the young subjects in this study was in the inquiry. Having completed the initial interpretation of the series, many of the children, especially the younger ones, were ready to turn to other activities. Considerable encouragement was necessary to persuade them to go through the cards a second time so that the investigator could locate more accurately the determinants of their responses. This difficulty was less serious than had been anticipated because the younger children usually gave much of the necessary inquiry information in their initial contact with the blot. That is, initial responses were accompanied by spontaneous gestures which quite clearly defined the area being interpreted. In many cases the inquiry seemed to prolong unnecessarily the test for both child and adult. The writer was tempted to omit the inquiry with the younger children but resisted this temptation in the interests of consistency.

Further study may indicate that a brief inquiry following each blot will increase the effectiveness of the test in its use with preschool children. Klopfer and Margulies (88) made this same suggestion but for another reason. They anticipated difficulty in the inquiry because they believed that young children would be unable to identify their first responses after completing the series. When they found that young children know almost as frequently and just as well what they had in mind as do adults, the suggestion was dropped. Bochner and Halpern also report difficulty with children in the inquiry. They say, "In addition to the language difficulty, the inquiry is often used by the child as an opportunity for making additional interpretations as well as giving free rein to his fantasy, rather than elucidating the original protocol. These difficulties may prove insurmountable, and a true inquiry may not be obtained. It is important, therefore, that the examiner watch the child when he gives his original responses in an effort to determine what part of the blot was used for interpretation." (26, page 104.) In this study very little difficulty was caused by the child's "giving free rein to his fantasy" although some cases did occur. In general, young children were more apt to tire of the material and were eager to make the inquiry as brief as possible.

The earliest age when Rorschach records are obtainable has not been determined. Since securing Rorschach records depends upon the willingness of the subject to cooperate, his ability to concentrate his attention on a specific task, and his ability to express his meanings in words, and since these abilities differ considerably in subjects of the same chronological age, it is almost impossible to set any definite age as the lower age limit of the test. Klopfer and Margulies (88) have assembled preschool records from various sources. Seventeen records of children between 2 and 3 years are included. These authors report having seen a few records of children under 2 years. In the present study 3 years was set as the lower age limit. Although it is possible to secure Rorschach records of gifted children under 3 years, the writer feels that these cases are exceptions and questions the value of using the Rorschach Test with the average child under 3 years. Even the most cooperative children between 2 and 3 years are handicapped by their limited ability to express themselves verbally.

In relation to the use of the Rorschach Test with very young children, Klopfer and Margulies (88) have defined three successive patterns of early Rorschach reactions:

A. "Magic repetition." The child repeats the same word in response to each card. This word may be determined by some rather vague impression received from the first card or it may have no relation even to the first card.

B. Modification of pattern A. The above pattern may be modified by:

1. Substitution of rejection as a "magic key." Some of the child's responses show at least a crude relation to the cards but he rejects, either silently or verbally, more than three of the cards.
2. Limited use of "magic repetition." Some of the child's responses show at least a crude relation to the cards, but he resorts to "magic repetition" in at least four of the cards. To be counted in this category the perseverated response must be to the card as a whole.

C. The majority of the cards—at least seven of the ten—are given a variety of responses which bear at least a crude relation to the card.

Klopfer and Margulies claim that pattern A is rare after 3 years and disappears completely after 4 years. Pattern B is common in the records of children between 2 and 4 years, tends to diminish in the records of children between 4 and 5 years, and is rare after 5 years. Pattern C is very rare before 3 years.

In order to check the above patterns, an attempt was made to identify them in the records in the present study. Pattern A was completely lacking in all records. This was to be expected since pattern A is said to be rare in records of children older than 3 years. One of the two forms of pattern B was identified in 18 of the 123 records. It appeared in 8 records of 3-year-olds, in 6 records of 4-year-olds, in 4 records of 5-year-olds, and not at all in the records of 6- and 7-year-olds. This finding is in line with the claims made except that the pattern was still present in the records of 6- and 7-year-olds. In Table 4 the

TABLE 4.—DISTRIBUTION OF EARLY REACTION PATTERNS A, B, AND C

AGE	KLOPFER AND MARGULIES							FORD						
		A		B		C			A		B		C	
	N*	N	%	N	%	N	%	N*	N	%	N	%	N	%
2-6 to 2-11	10	4	40	6	60	...	...	...	...	...	...	...	...	...
3-0 to 3-11	27	3	11	9	33	15	56	25	...	...	8	32	17	68
4-0 to 4-11	32	...	...	5	16	27	84	27	...	...	6	22	21	78
5-0 to 5-11	24	...	...	1	4	23	96	25	...	...	4	16	21	84
6-0 to 6-11	...	...	...	...	...	...	...	23	...	...	...	...	23	100
7-0 to 7-11	...	...	...	...	...	...	...	23	...	...	...	...	23	100

* *N*=total number of records at each age level.

data from the Klopfer and Margulies study and the present study are compared. In interpreting this table it is important to keep in mind that the subjects in these two studies, while comparable with each other, are not representative of the population in general. The children were well above average in intelligence and socio-economic status. It is almost certain, therefore, that their reaction patterns are more mature than those of average children of the same age. For this reason the age when patterns A and B tend to disappear is probably underestimated, as is the age when pattern C may be expected to appear.

In addition to the three early reaction patterns suggested by Klopfer and Margulies, another pattern appeared often enough in the records of the present study to merit further investigation. In this new pattern some of the child's responses show at least a crude relation to the cards, but he resorts to "magic repetition" in at least 4 of the cards, although these perseverated responses are referred to details of the blots. In pattern B the perseverated responses are counted as such only when they are given to the card as a whole. In the new pattern the child is far enough along in his development of logical concepts to feel inhibited in the indiscriminate use of "magic repetition," but he cannot yet give up this useful mode of response. Consequently, once he has given a response which catches his fancy, he holds to this "magic key" and looks for parts of the blot to which he can apply it without undue violation to his increasing understanding of logical relationships. For example, in card III the center red blot may be interpreted quite logically as a butterfly. Pleased with the word, or sensing the fitness of his response, the child may perseverate the concept and look for details in the cards that follow to which he may apply the response "butterfly." This pattern was identified in 4 (16 per cent) of the records of 3-year-olds, 3 (11 per cent) of the records of 4-year-olds, 2 (8 per cent) of the records of 5-year-olds, 2 (9 per cent) of the records of 6-year-olds, and in none of the records of 7-year-olds.

Analysis of early reaction patterns as revealed by the Rorschach Test suggests four rather distinct stages:

1. The pre-logic stage, which is identical except in name with Klopfer and Margulies' "magic repetition" pattern.

2. The confused-logic stage, which is identical with Klopfer and Margulies' modification of magic repetition pattern.

3. The perseverated-logic stage, described in the preceding paragraph.

4. The true-logic stage, which is identical with Klopfer and Margulies' pattern C.

These stages are tentative and have more theoretical than practical value since they have little to do with the interpretation of test results. They do, however, suggest the possibility of using the Rorschach technique for the study of the genetic development of logical concepts.

VIII. MEANS OF THE RORSCHACH TEST DETERMINANTS

One of the major difficulties involved in the use of the Rorschach Test with young children at the present time is the lack of norms on which to base interpretations. To the writer's knowledge only three articles have been published which deal primarily with the presentation of data from Rorschach records of American children younger than 8 years.* Paulsen (112) studied a group of 82 children ranging in age between 5 years 11 months and 6 years 10 months. Her discussion of the data is brief and, except for average number of total responses, no actual norms are given. Sunne (135) studied a group of 4435 first-grade white, Negro, and southern mountain children, but her article is so concerned with the comparison of the content of the responses of the three groups that norms for the more important test determinants are completely lacking. Klopfer and Margulies (88) studied the records of 205 preschool children ranging in age between 2 and 7 years. This was not a normative study since the group was composed, for the most part, of children of superior mental ability who came from higher than average socio-economic backgrounds. Means of various test determinants were reported.

The present study is not a normative one. Like those in the Klopfer and Margulies study, these children represent a highly selected group both in intelligence and in socio-economic status. The means of the Rorschach test determinants presented in this chapter are meaningful only in relation to a highly selected segment of the total population of comparable age. Only as various other clearly defined groups of children are studied and the records compared will it be possible to define Rorschach norms for young children. Means of the test determinants at the five age levels included in this study are presented in Table 5.

Responses

A study of Table 5 and Figure 2 indicates that the mean number of responses increases slowly but steadily between

* Since the completion of this study five papers have been published on various aspects of the use of the Rorschach Test with young children (46, 69, 75, 124, and 150).

Table 5.—Means of the Rorschach Test Determinants in Relation to Chronological Age

Age	*3 years*		*4 years*		*5 years*		*6 years*		*7 years*	
Subjects	*25*		*27*		*25*		*23*		*23*	
DETERMINANT	MEAN	SD	MEAN	SD	MEAN	SD	MEAN	SD	MEAN	SD
R	15.6	6.10	16.3	6.55	17.2	4.94	24.4	6.17	30.6	11.52
Obj	20.5	9.62	24.0	11.05	24.0	7.31	35.5	11.73	47.6	18.06
OL	9.1	6.54	12.8	10.38	15.1	7.49	26.7	15.23	37.0	17.99
Reaction time										
Gray blots	8.1	7.37	7.7	3.20	10.8	8.39	10.7	5.86	10.3	6.79
Colored blots	8.5	8.94	8.3	4.86	11.0	10.00	10.5	4.62	8.6	4.79
Average	8.3	8.08	8.0	3.40	10.9	8.90	10.6	5.17	9.6	5.31
W (W, DW, WS)	5.0	1.31	5.6	2.17	5.4	2.20	5.8	2.57	6.0	3.35
D	8.6	4.68	8.7	4.83	10.2	4.44	15.0	5.45	19.3	7.94
Dr	0.8	1.20	1.0	1.43	0.9	1.03	2.1	2.01	4.4	4.53
Dr, Do, DS	2.0	2.04	1.9	2.18	1.6	1.92	3.6	2.60	5.4	4.92
%W (W, DW, WS) *	37.0	18.33	38.9	17.02	33.3	13.69	25.2	12.80	22.8	14.40
%D	51.9	17.90	51.6	14.46	58.7	15.10	60.5	12.20	61.9	9.28
%Dr	4.4	6.31	5.0	6.33	4.4	5.01	8.1	7.41	12.0	7.91
%Dr, Do, DS	11.0	9.89	9.7	9.12	8.2	9.15	14.3	10.54	15.3	10.54
F	13.5	5.51	12.9	5.23	12.5	4.53	17.9	6.00	22.7	9.44
F+	5.6	3.73	7.2	3.59	7.0	2.79	12.1	5.24	15.8	6.66
M (M, FM, m)	0.8	1.10	1.5	1.89	2.6	2.17	3.6	3.50	4.8	3.08
M+ (M, FM, m)	0.6	0.85	1.0	1.47	2.1	1.72	2.9	2.96	4.0	2.66
C, CF, FC	1.2	1.60	1.8	1.51	2.0	1.55	2.2	2.09	3.0	2.31
%F	86.0	11.60	80.5	14.22	73.8	17.13	73.4	14.03	73.8	11.32
%F+†	39.0	18.06	56.7	17.71	60.2	22.26	66.4	10.80	70.2	11.17
%M (M, FM, m)	5.1	7.25	8.0	10.19	14.9	12.85	14.4	12.65	17.0	9.92
%M+ (M, FM, m)‡	30.3	43.01	35.3	43.00	66.4	39.02	69.4	40.69	80.0	26.06
%C, CF, FC	7.8	11.09	10.5	8.26	11.1	8.21	9.1	8.66	7.2	6.41
C-sum	1.1	1.38	1.5	1.29	1.9	1.87	2.1	2.04	2.1	2.22
A (A, Ad)	7.0	5.38	8.0	4.20	9.0	3.66	12.6	3.32	15.6	6.69
%A (A, Ad)	43.1	29.13	51.5	29.01	51.9	16.57	54.1	19.01	53.0	14.14
H (H, Hd)	1.9	2.01	2.1	2.35	1.4	2.03	3.4	2.47	5.0	3.47
%H (H, Hd)	13.0	13.05	12.2	11.02	8.6	10.59	13.2	8.86	16.8	9.81
Content range	4.8	2.04	4.8	2.03	5.4	2.07	7.0	2.90	8.0	3.06
P	1.4	1.20	2.5	1.75	3.7	1.77	4.5	1.77	5.4	1.66
%P	9.2	7.34	16.4	12.25	25.1	12.32	20.0	9.60	20.2	10.70
O	1.0	5.04	1.3	1.70	1.8	1.50	3.1	2.33	3.2	2.18
%O	4.8	5.40	6.4	7.78	15.1	7.49	12.3	8.36	9.9	6.10

* Unless otherwise stated, percentages are in terms of total R.

† %F+=F+/F.

‡ %M+=M+/M.

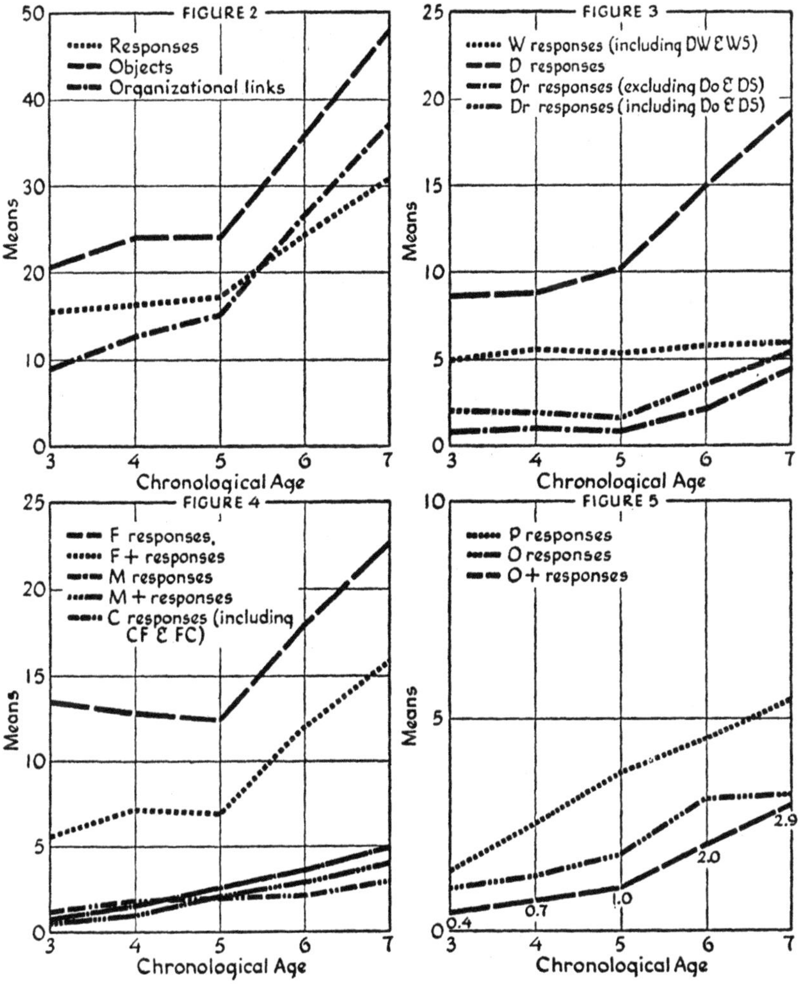

Figure 2.—Mean Number of Responses, Objects, and Organizational Links in Relation to Chronological Age. *Figure 3.*—Manner of Apperception in Relation to Chronological Age (Mean Number of W, D, Dr Excluding Do and DS, and Dr Including Do and DS). *Figure 4.*—Quality of the Response in Relation to Chronological Age (Mean Number of F, F+, M, M+, and Color Responses). *Figure 5.*—Mean Number of P, O, and O+ Responses in Relation to Chronological Age.

3 and 5 years. At 6 years there is a decided increase in number of responses. This increase continues at approximately the same rate between 6 and 7 years. These findings are similar to those reported by Klopfer and Margulies for comparable age groups except that the mean is somewhat higher for the 6-year-olds in this study. It is also higher than the mean reported by Paulsen for the children in her study. A comparison of the mean number of responses in these three investigations seems to indicate that the decision to eliminate rotation of the cards in the present study did not result in a decrease in number of interpretations.

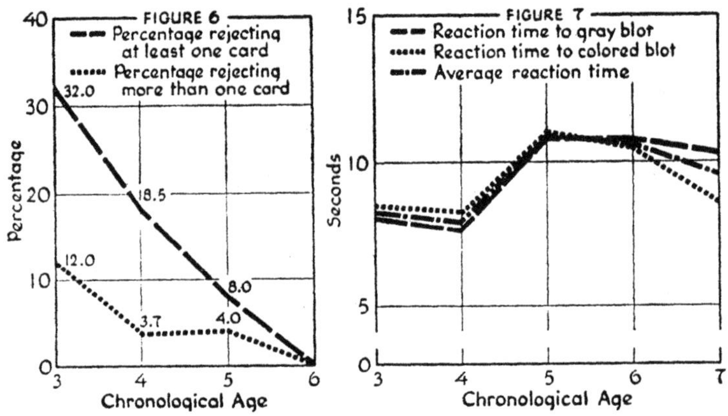

Figure 6.—Percentage of Children Rejecting Cards. *Figure 7.*—Reaction Time for Responses to the Rorschach Cards.

Rejections

Figure 6 shows the percentage of children rejecting at least one card and also the percentage rejecting more than one card. This second comparison is included because rejection of two cards is the usual limit set for the normal adult record. In each case the percentage of rejection drops sharply with increasing age. No child over 6 years of age rejected any of the cards. These figures are in close agreement with those reported by Klopfer and Margulies.

Objects

The increase with age in the number of objects named is similar to the increase in responses (Table 5 and Figure 2).

Since many of the objects were included within a response, the mean total objects is always greater than the mean total number of responses.

Organizational Links

Table 5 and Figure 2 indicate that the average number of organizational links within responses increases somewhat more rapidly between 3 and 5 years but, as in responses and objects named, the marked increase occurs at 6 years.

Reaction Time

The interval between presentation of the card and the first response is called the reaction time. As indicated in Table 5 and Figure 7, the children in this study showed relatively little variation in average reaction time. There are no comparable figures for other groups of young children, but Hertz (57) reported an average reaction time of 10.71 seconds (*SD* 6.75) for her adolescent group. Reaction times for children between 8 and 12 years have not been reported. The average reaction time to the gray blots (I, IV, V, VI, VII) shows a very slight tendency to be lower than the average reaction time to the colored blots (II, III, VIII, IX, X) at 3, 4, and 5 years. At 6 and 7 years, however, the average reaction time is higher for the gray than for the colored blots. Since this difference is slight, it is probably a function of the particular group in this study rather than a characteristic of young children in general.

Manner of Apperception

Because the determinants descriptive of manner of apperception depend to a large extent upon the determinants descriptive of the quality of the response, any comparison which separates these determinants distorts the total picture. For example, the quick response given by very young children is often vaguely referred to the whole blot. The quality of this response is apt to be poor, and it is extremely difficult to tell whether the response is predominantly determined by the whole blot (W) or whether some detail is the basis of the interpretation which is referred by the child to the whole (DW). When W responses are given by older children, they are usually less vague, often good form, and sometimes clearly indicative of real effort to integrate the various parts of the blot into the response. In spite of these difficulties it seems desirable to present in Table 5 and Figures 3 and 8 a comparison of the relative incidence of the determinants descriptive of manner of apperception or mode of response.

In terms of absolute numbers, W responses, including DW and WS responses, show little variation with age. Since the distinction between W and DW responses in the records of very young children is often impossible and usually open to question, DW responses are included in W responses. Also included in W responses are WS responses, since their occurrence was too infrequent to justify a separate category. The incidence of Do and DS responses was also too infrequent to justify separate classification, so these responses are included in Dr responses. Figure 3 indicates that Dr responses, both including and excluding Do and DS responses, show little variation with age between 3 and 5 years. Between 5 and 6 years the number increases, and it continues to increase between 6 and 7 years. D responses show similar characteristics. They are relatively constant between 3 and 5 years but show a marked increase between 5 and 7 years. The increase in D and Dr responses between 5 and 7 years is primarily responsible for the increase in total number of responses between these ages. That is, children between 5 and 7 years tend to give more interpretations based on details and rare details than do younger children, and by so doing they increase the number of their responses.

The findings in this study do not agree with those of Klopfer and Margulies, who report a relatively high incidence among preschool children of records in which the mode of response is 100 per cent W. In the present study no record contained 100 per cent W responses. Figure 8 indicates that the percentage of W responses is relatively constant between 3 and 4 years and decreases between 4 and 7 years. This decrease is more marked between 4 and 6 years than between 6 and 7 years. The percentage of D responses is relatively constant between 3 and 4 years, increases between 4 and 5 years, and is again relatively constant between 5 and 7 years. The percentage of Dr responses is relatively constant between 3 and 5 years but increases somewhat between 5 and 7 years.

Quality of the Response

Table 5 and Figures 4 and 9 indicate that most of the interpretations at each age level are based on form. The average

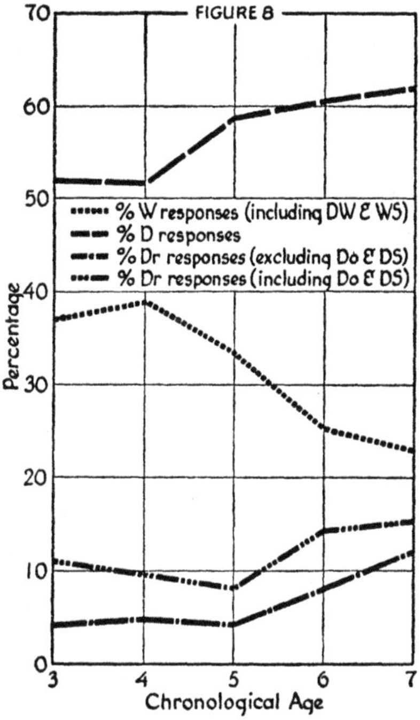

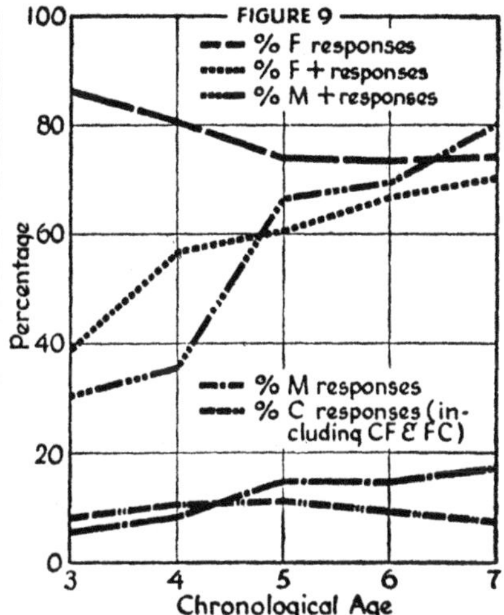

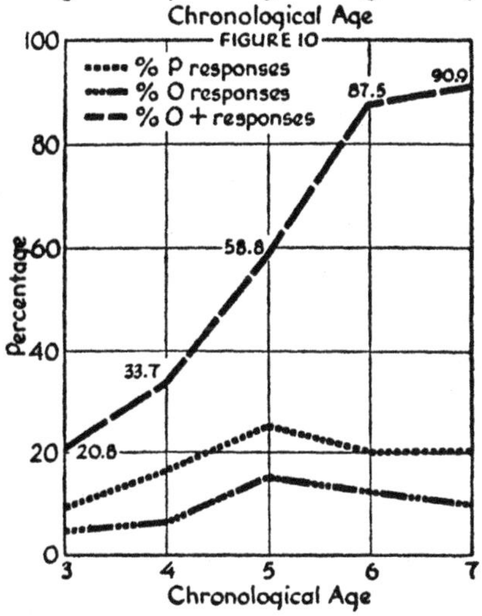

Figure 8.—MANNER OF APPERCEPTION IN RELATION TO CHRONOLOGICAL AGE (PERCENTAGE OF W, D, DR EXCLUDING DO AND DS, AND DR INCLUDING DO AND DS). *Figure 9.*—QUALITY OF THE RESPONSE IN RELATION TO CHRONOLOGICAL AGE (PERCENTAGE OF F, F+, M, M+, AND COLOR RESPONSES). *Figure 10.*—PERCENTAGE OF P, O, AND O+ RESPONSES IN RELATION TO CHRONOLOGICAL AGE.

number of F responses is relatively constant between 3 and 5 years but increases rapidly between 5 and 7 years. In terms of percentage of total R, F responses decrease between 3 and 5 years but remain relatively constant between 5 and 7 years. M responses, in terms both of average and of percentage of total R, tend to increase slowly but steadily with increasing age, while color responses remain relatively constant throughout the age groups. The average number of F+ and M+ responses increases with age, as shown in Figure 9, where F+ and M+ responses are calculated in terms of percentage of total number of F and M responses respectively.

Each subject in this investigation based some of his interpretations on form, but relatively few gave responses in which motion or color was the primary determinant. Some records also showed shading responses (K) and color-naming responses (Cn). There is general agreement among Rorschach workers that K responses, often referred to as Y responses, are infrequent in the records of young children. The evidence here supports this assumption, since each age group averaged less than one K response. However, K responses were present even in the records of some 3-year-olds, and the percentage of children giving K responses increased markedly after 5 years.* Cn responses are seldom found in the records of normal individuals, and it is generally agreed that they indicate some abnormality. In the light of this hypothesis, it is interesting to find that 48 per cent of the 3-year-olds in this study gave Cn responses. The percentage of children giving Cn responses decreased from 33 at 4 years to 25 at 5 years. No Cn responses appeared in the records of children after 6 years of age.

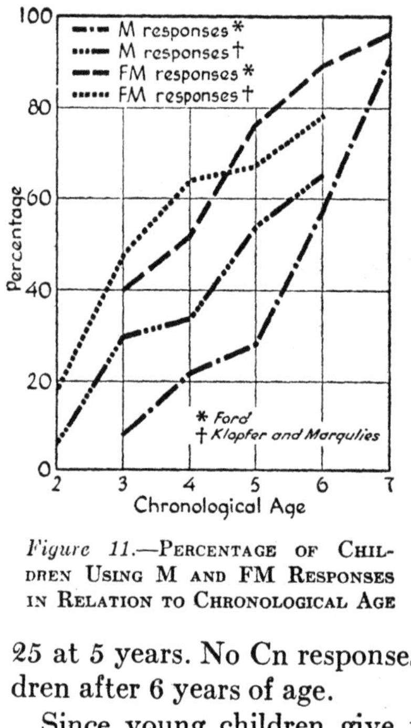

Figure 11.—PERCENTAGE OF CHILDREN USING M AND FM RESPONSES IN RELATION TO CHRONOLOGICAL AGE

Since young children give relatively few motion and color responses, the percentage of children giving each response was calculated. In order to compare these figures with the ones reported by Klopfer and Margulies, movement responses were divided into M, FM, and m, and color responses were divided into C, CF, and FC. Table 6 and Figure 11 indicate that the percentage of children using M and FM increases rapidly with increasing age. At each age level the percentage using FM is greater than the percentage using M. Although the percentage at each level is lower than that reported by Klopfer and Margulies, the evidence of this study supports their claim that

* K responses were given by 14 per cent of the 3-year-olds, 16 per cent of the 4-year-olds, 23 per cent of the 5-year-olds, 34 per cent of the 6-year-olds, and 42 per cent of the 7-year-olds.

movement responses appear in the records of preschool children and increase in frequency with increasing age. In both studies the incidence of m responses was too infrequent and too irregular to warrant any interpretation at the preschool level.

Table 6 and Figure 12 indicate that the percentage of children giving CF responses is higher than the percentage giving FC and C responses except at the 5-year level, where the percentage of children giving FC responses is higher. The percentage giving C responses shows a steady increase within the age levels included in this study. The percentage giving CF responses increases between 3 and 4, decreases at 5, increases at 6, and remains relatively constant between 6 and 7 years. The percentage of children giving FC responses increases between 3 and 5 and is relatively constant between 5 and 7 years.

TABLE 6.—PERCENTAGE OF CHILDREN GIVING MOVEMENT AND COLOR RESPONSES IN RELATION TO CHRONOLOGICAL AGE

AGE	FORD							KLOPFER AND MARGULIES						
	N*	M	FM	m	FC	CF	C	N*	M	FM	m	FC	CF	C
2-0 to 2-11	0	...	...	...	...	...	...	?	6	18	18	12	12	29
3-0 to 3-11	25	8	40	0	28	32	12	?	30	48	2	37	24	46
4-0 to 4-11	27	22	52	0	44	56	15	?	34	64	9	27	45	30
5-0 to 5-11	25	28	76	16	56	36	36	?	54	67	13	54	67	41
6-0 to 6-11	23	57	89	4	57	61	35	?	65	78	9	65	43	30
7-0 to 7-11	23	91	96	0	52	57	43	0	...	...	...	...	...	...

* N=total number of records at each age level.

These results differ from those of Klopfer and Margulies, who report that C responses predominate between 2 and 4, CF responses between 4 and 5, and FC responses at 6 years. These findings are in line with the generally accepted interpretation that C responses are indicative of uninhibited emotionality, CF responses of a tendency of emotions to predominate, and FC responses of emotional adjustment. According to this hypothesis, one would expect C responses to decrease during very early childhood, CF responses to decrease, but less rapidly than C responses, and FC responses to show a steady increase. One possible explanation for the low incidence of C responses in the records of the present study is the fact that Cn responses were not included in C responses, whereas they were included in the Klopfer and Margulies study. As indicated earlier in this chapter, Cn responses are relatively frequent between 2 and 5 years but tend to drop out after 6 years. Thus the addition of

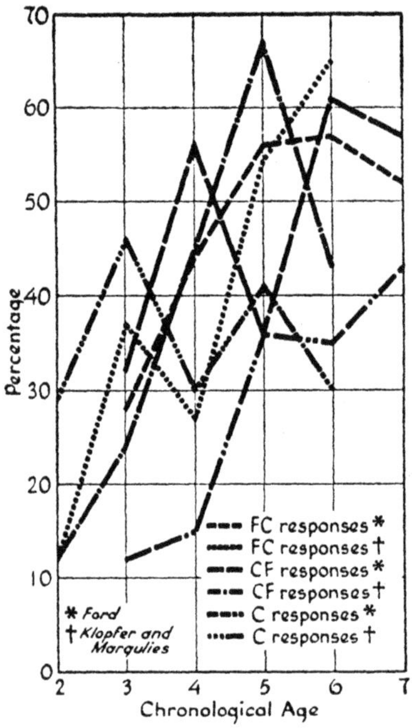

Figure 12.—PERCENTAGE OF CHILDREN USING FC, CF, AND C RESPONSES IN RELATION TO CHRONOLOGICAL AGE

Cn responses would increase C responses, especially at 3 years, and would result in the predominance of C responses at the 3-year level. With the exception of the predominance of FC responses at 5 years, CF responses predominate in the records of the young children in this study. This is in agreement with the findings of Paulsen that CF responses continue to predominate at the 7-year level and seems to indicate that the predominance of FC over CF responses, in terms both of means (see Table 7) and of the percentage of children using the determinant, occurs sometime after the seventh year. It is not in agreement with the findings of Klopfer and Margulies, who report that FC responses predominate at the 6-year level.

TABLE 7.—MEANS FOR M, FM, m, FC, CF, C, Cn, AND K RESPONSES IN RELATION TO CHRONOLOGICAL AGE

Age	*3 years*	*4 years*	*5 years*	*6 years*	*7 years*
Subjects	*25*	*27*	*25*	*23*	*23*
DETERMINANT					
M	0.1	0.3	0.5	1.2	2.4
FM	0.7	1.2	2.0	2.4	2.4
m	0.0	0.0	0.1	0.1	0.0
FC	0.5	0.8	0.8	0.7	1.1
CF	0.5	0.8	0.5	1.0	1.2
C	0.2	0.2	0.8	0.5	0.7
Cn	0.7	0.7	0.4	0.0	0.0
K	0.2	0.2	0.2	0.7	0.7

CONTENT OF THE RESPONSE

The content of the responses shows little variation with age except that with increasing age a wider range of content appears.

Table 5 shows that the mean content classifications increases from 4.8 at 3 years to 8.00 at 7 years. Between 5 and 7 years nature responses tend to decrease and an increase is noted in responses interpreted as fairies, elves, dragons, and other imaginary characters. This is consistent with the interest children of this age show in fairy tales, and it is not surprising to find this interest reflected in inkblot interpretations.

Table 8 shows the mean percentage of responses falling within the content categories. A detailed list of the items within the various content categories will be found in Appendix A. Just as animal responses are most frequently given by adults,

TABLE 8.—MEAN PERCENTAGE OF RESPONSES WITHIN THE VARIOUS CONTENT CATEGORIES IN RELATION TO CHRONOLOGICAL AGE

Age	*3 years*	*4 years*	*5 years*	*6 years*	*7 years*
Subjects	*25*	*27*	*25*	*23*	*23*
CONTENT CATEGORY					
Animal	36	48	45	42	40
Animal detail	7	3	7	12	13
Human	10	7	6	8	11
Human detail	3	5	3	5	6
Nature	18	17	16	8	6
Objects	7	5	3	4	3
Food and clothing	4	3	4	7	6
Toys	3	2	3	2	2
Architecture	4	5	4	3	2
Landscape and seascape	3	3	5	7	6
Anatomy	1	1	3	1	2
Art	4	1	1	1	3

they are also most frequent in the records of young children. Table 5 indicates that although the mean frequency of animal responses increases with increasing age, the %A (including %Ad) is consistently around 50. With three exceptions, all at the 3-year level, each child in this study gave at least one A response. The second most frequent category of the content range is nature. Within this category trees are mentioned more frequently than any other item. Flowers, leaves, fire, clouds, sun, and snow are also frequent nature interpretations. These findings are in agreement with those of Sunne, who reported that animal and nature constituted the two major content categories. Although Sunne reported anatomy as a third major category, the findings of the present study indicate that human responses, including imaginary, humanlike characters, are third in terms of frequency. Perhaps one explanation of this difference is the fact that the writer was careful in her inquiry to seek further explanation when responses such as leg, arm, foot, and the like were given. On the surface such responses appeared to be anatomical interpretations, but in most cases the child's further explanation revealed that they were more truly animal or human detail responses. True anatomical responses are relatively rare in the records of the children in this investigation.

In addition to the major categories of animal, nature, and human, seven minor categories are mentioned with varying frequency. Within the object category the most frequently mentioned items are household furniture (beds, chairs, candles, and flowerpots), means of transportation (boats, trains, and airplanes), and implements (sticks, guns, and saws). Ice cream and hair ribbons are the most popular items under food and clothing. Landscape and seascape interpretations are concerned mainly with mountains, rocks, water, and oceans. Most frequently mentioned in the toy category are jack-o'-lanterns, balls, snowmen, and paper dolls. In the architecture category, interest centers around houses, castles, and bridges. Blood is the principal item in the anatomy category, but brains, insides of stomachs, and skeletons are mentioned several times. Between 3 and 5 years the art responses are mostly "paint" but after 5 years the principal items are statues, decorations, and designs.

In general, the young children projected into the content of their interpretations those things with which normal young children of this age are concerned. In some cases, the content could be traced to the individual child's recent experiences, such as a visit to the circus or the zoo. Several children revealed through the explanation of their responses areas of concern and anxiety. For example, when asked about the response, "Shadows, just dark shadows," one little boy explained, "Like when mommy turns out the light and I go to bed. The shadows come." Later conversation with the child's mother revealed that he had recently "put on an awful scene at bedtime for no reason at all." When asked if he had ever mentioned shadows the mother said, "No, I've never heard him use the word." Then after a minute's hesitation she continued, "Oh, several months ago he used to get out of bed and come downstairs. His daddy told him the shadows would get him if he didn't stay in bed, but he has forgotten all that. He doesn't get out of bed any more once we get him in." So the "forgotten" experience revealed in Rorschach content was the key to disturbing behavior for which there was "no reason at all."

Popular Responses

No attempt was made in this study to separate content on the basis of parts of the blot responded to.* It was noted, however, that certain blots or parts of blots stimulated similar responses. For example, the whole of card II was frequently interpreted as "butterfly" and the pink side blots on card VIII were almost always seen as animals—usually bears. Both these examples are popular responses for adults and were so scored in the children's records. Unfortunately the small number of cases made it impossible to set up a clearly defined category of P responses for young children. Scored on the basis of P responses in adults, the number of P responses in this study increases slightly but steadily with increasing age, as is indicated in Table 5 and Figure 5. Table 5 and Figure 10 indicate that the ratio of P responses to total responses increases between 3 and 5 years, decreases slightly at 6 years, and remains relatively constant between 6 and 7 years. In other words, when P is defined in terms of the adult norm the percentage increases with chronological age.

Original Responses

Table 5 and Figure 5 indicate that the number of O responses increases slightly with increasing age. Figure 10 shows that %O also increases between 3 and 5 years but decreases between 5 and 7 years. Original responses based on good form (O+), in terms both of means and of percentages (%O+ = O+/O), show a steady increase with increasing age. Therefore it would seem that the decrease in mean O responses between 5 and 7 years is due primarily to the dropping out of infantile original responses which were based on poor form (O—).

Other Studies

Comparison of the means of the various Rorschach determinants for the young children in this study and those of comparable age groups reported by Paulsen, Sunne, and Klopfer and Margulies was made whenever possible throughout this chapter and will be mentioned only incidentally in this section. In Table

* A detailed analysis of content in relation to the part of the blot interpreted will be published separately.

9 the norms for various other age groups are summarized and compared with those in the present study. This comparison does not aim to be exhaustive; its purpose is to select from the literature certain representative studies and, through the comparison of the reported results, to point out changes in the test determinants which seem to be related to age. For this purpose

TABLE 9.—RORSCHACH NORMS IN RELATION TO CHRONOLOGICAL AGE *

Investigator.	*Rorschach*	*Hertz* †	*Behn-Eschenburg*	*Lopfe*	*Loosli-Usteri*	*Kerr*	*Ford*	
Subjects.....	*?*	*300*	*209*	*120*	*63*	*40* ‡	*46*	*77*
Age.........	*Adults*	*12 to 16*	*13 to 15*	*10 to 13*	*10 to 12*	*7 to 8*	*6 to 8*	*3 to 6*
DETERMINANT								
R	15 to 30	27.1	33.6	42.0	23	26.0	27.5	16.3
W	4 to 7	6.8	5.8	3.7	5	2.5	5.9	5.3
D		14.1	18.4	19.0	15	21.9	17.1	9.2
Dr		1.9	7.1	13.5	2		3.3	0.9
Do		1.0	0.9	1.5	0		0.7	0.6
DS		1.7	1.0	2.3	1	1.2	0.5	0.3
%F+	70 to 80%	88.8%	71%	75%	80%		68.3%	52.1%
M	2 to 4	2.6	1.3	0.9	0	1.0	4.2	1.6
							1.8§	0.3§
C	0		0.1	0.7	0	0.1	0.6	0.4
CF	0 to 1		0.4	1.1	1	0.7	1.1	0.6
FC	1 to 3		1.5	1.3	1	0.4	0.9	0.7
C-sum	0.5 to 2.5	1.3	1.3	2.7	1		2.1	1.5
%A	30 to 55%	54.1%	47%	55%	57%	54.3%	53.6%	48.6%
%P		25.6%		11%	21%	18.4%	20.1%	16.9%
%O	0 to 20%	6.8%		25%			11.1%	8.7%

* Unless indicated by %, all figures are in terms of absolute numbers.
† Hertz's figures rounded to one decimal.
‡ Girls only.
§ Means for M excluding FM and m responses.

the records of children who were 3, 4, and 5 years old are combined to constitute a preschool group, and the records of the 6- and 7-year-olds are combined into a second group. Not all the test determinants discussed in this chapter are included, since comparable data from other studies was lacking.

There is considerable variation in the means reported by the several investigators whose studies are included in Table 9. Part of this variation may be due to differences in administering and scoring the test. A second factor which may contribute to differences in the reported norms is nationality. Swiss (Rorschach, Behn-Eschenburg, Lopfe, and Loosli-Usteri), English (Kerr), and American (Hertz and Ford) children are represented in these studies. These two factors, in addition to the fact that the subjects in the present study were superior in intelligence and socio-economic background to average children of comparable age, should be kept in mind throughout the following discussion.

Table 9 indicates that the mean R for the preschool children in this study is considerably lower than that for the 6- and 7-year-olds. The mean R for the older children is similar not only to the mean reported by Kerr for a comparable age group, but also to the mean reported by Hertz for adolescents. Since the data of Klopfer and Margulies give a very similar mean-R (16.9) for their total preschool group, these findings suggest that the total number of responses increases with increasing age during the preschool years but reaches the adult level sometime between 6 and 8 years—perhaps slightly later in average children.

There is almost no difference between the mean W for the preschool group and that for the older group in this study. Both means are higher than that reported by Kerr and only slightly under that reported by Hertz. Since all the means are within the range suggested by Rorschach for normal adults, this comparison suggests that W is, as claimed by Rorschach, unrelated to age.

A marked increase is apparent in the mean D between the two groups in the present study. Although the mean D for the 6- and 7-year-olds is slightly under that reported by Kerr,* it is quite comparable to the means reported by Behn-Eschenburg, Lopfe, and Loosli-Usteri and somewhat above that reported by Hertz. The increase in R between the preschool and early school years may be attributed largely to an increase in D responses. A slight tendency for Dr to increase with age in the present study is noted, but the evidence from the several studies is conflicting. All investigators agree that Do and DS responses are relatively rare in Rorschach records. The difference is slight but consistent enough to suggest that Do and DS responses may increase very gradually with increasing age.

The findings in this study, in agreement with those reported by Klopfer and Margulies, suggest that %F+ increases with increasing age. Comparison with the means for the adolescent groups suggests that this increase continues, but less rapidly, at the older age levels. Although the mean for the 6- and 7-

* This is to be expected because Kerr included Dr in her D responses.

year-olds is almost within the lower limit of %F+ set by Rorschach for normal adults, it is considerably lower than the mean reported by Hertz for adolescents.

In this study the mean of M (including FM) responses is higher for the 6- and 7-year-olds than for the preschool children. The mean for the older groups is also higher than that reported by any other investigator. Since all the investigators, including the writer, used Rorschach's instructions in scoring M responses, this difference cannot be attributed to the fact that FM responses are included in M responses. The greater frequency of M, however, may be due to the superior intellectual level of the group, since M is claimed to be closely related to intelligence. This hypothesis will be tested in Chapter XI.

In agreement with Klopfer and Margulies, this investigation indicates the presence of a few C responses in the records of young children. Hertz does not give comparable figures, but the other investigators, except for Rorschach and Loosli-Usteri, report the presence of a few C responses. Rorschach and Loosli-Usteri claimed that C responses are not present in the records of adults and older children. The present study does not agree with the studies of Klopfer and Margulies and the other investigators in finding relatively more CF than FC responses. This difference may be due to age. That is, as Paulsen suggested, CF responses may predominate beyond the age limit included in the present study. However, the differences are so slight that any hypothesis as to their meaning is questionable. Since C-sum is dependent upon the frequency of C, CF, and FC responses, and since more of these responses are present in the records of this study, it is not surprising to find the C-sum higher here than in other studies.

The percentage of A responses, though slightly less for the preschool group than for the older children, is quite similar to that reported by other investigators, all of whom report %A within the range established by Rorschach for normal adults. This suggests that %A is relatively constant for all age levels above 6 years.

Results here indicate a slight increase in %P with increasing age. The %P reported by Kerr is slightly lower than that for the older group in this study. Hertz's %P, higher than that for the 6- and 7-year-olds in this study, suggests that %P may increase very gradually with increasing age. However, the lower mean reported by Lopfe leaves this hypothesis open to question.

In this study %O for both groups is lower than that reported by Lopfe but higher than that reported by Hertz. Both means are within the range of %O established by Rorschach for normal adults. The fact that the means here are higher than the mean reported by Hertz may again be due to the superior intellectual level of the subjects, since %O is said to be related to intelligence.

IX. SEX DIFFERENCES IN TEST DETERMINANTS

On the question of sex differences in test determinants there has been much speculation and relatively little research. Rorschach maintained that the number of whole responses tended to be lower and the number of color responses higher in the records of women than in the records of men. Klopfer and Kelley (87) claim that girls not only utilize the elementary color responses, C and CF, earlier but that they also utilize FC responses earlier. Paulsen (112) and Stavrianos (133) present evidence that supports the above claims. In addition, Paulsen says that boys give more movement responses than girls, while Stavrianos claims that girls utilize M responses earlier than boys.

In order to compare sex differences in the records of young children and to test the above hypotheses, the subjects in the present study were divided into two groups, a preschool group and a 6- and 7-year-old group. Although it would seem important to compare each age group separately in order to determine how and when sex changes in determinants occur, the small number of cases made it desirable to divide the data into no more than two groups. Table 10 shows the means and standard deviations for the boys and girls in the two groups. Two facts are quite evident: The similarity between means within each age group is marked, and in all cases the variation within a sex group is considerably greater than the slight differences which appear between the means of the various determinants. In terms of mean number and mean percentage of occurrence, the evidence here does not support the claims of previous writers concerning sex differences in test determinants. It should be pointed out that Paulsen also found that the individual differences within a sex group were greater than the differences between sex groups. Stavrianos, however, reported only the differences between groups without giving any indication of the variation within groups.

It seems to the writer that much of the confusion in regard to sex differences in Rorschach test determinants results from the failure to differentiate between two questions. First, there is the question of quantity. That is, are there any sex differences in

TABLE 10.—SEX DIFFERENCES IN TEST DETERMINANTS

Age	*3-0 to 5-11*				*6-0 to 7-11*			
Sex	*Boys*		*Girls*		*Boys*		*Girls*	
Subjects	*36*		*41*		*21*		*25*	
DETERMINANT	MEAN	SD	MEAN	SD	MEAN	SD	MEAN	SD
R	16.8	6.09	15.9	5.74	29.0	10.82	26.3	8.68
Obj	23.5	9.64	22.3	9.56	44.0	14.68	40.2	16.49
OL	12.3	9.00	12.4	8.73	33.3	16.67	30.6	17.97
Reaction time								
Gray blots	8.3	6.51	9.3	10.15	8.5	4.58	12.1	7.89
Colored blots	9.4	7.72	9.0	8.71	8.8	4.51	10.2	4.57
Average	8.9	6.19	9.1	7.63	8.7	4.13	11.2	5.69
W (W, DW, WS)	5.3	2.19	5.3	1.75	6.2	2.55	5.6	3.34
D	9.4	4.79	9.0	4.64	18.0	8.01	16.4	6.22
Dr	1.0	0.91	0.8	1.12	3.5	4.61	3.1	2.69
Dr, Do, DS	2.1	2.15	1.7	1.97	4.8	5.16	4.3	3.15
%W (W, DW, WS)*	35.9	12.48	36.0	13.88	25.2	11.94	23.0	11.89
%D	53.4	16.56	54.5	13.67	60.4	10.59	61.9	10.83
%Dr	5.0	6.05	4.3	5.81	9.6	8.31	10.5	7.75
%Dr, Do, DS	10.9	9.49	8.6	4.92	14.2	11.52	15.0	8.92
F	13.7	5.22	12.3	4.96	20.9	9.03	19.7	7.38
F+	7.3	3.42	6.0	3.36	14.7	6.98	13.4	5.45
M (M, FM, m)	1.6	1.56	1.6	2.26	4.7	3.55	3.8	3.03
M+ (M, FM, m)	1.3	1.40	1.2	1.66	4.0	3.20	3.0	2.47
C, CF, FC	1.3	1.47	2.0	1.62	3.1	2.10	2.2	1.55
%F	81.8	12.78	78.7	17.20	72.1	11.76	74.8	13.44
%F+†	53.7	18.54	50.6	23.59	68.5	10.54	68.1	11.81
%M (M, FM, m)	10.0	9.63	8.7	14.92	16.7	11.62	14.9	10.79
%M+ (M, FM, m)‡	50.8	45.02	37.7	43.39	81.3	40.38	69.1	36.67
%C, CF, FC	7.3	7.23	12.1	10.12	8.9	8.04	7.5	6.29
C-sum	1.2	1.39	1.8	1.65	2.5	2.89	1.7	2.28
A (A, Ad)	8.8	3.33	7.3	6.68	14.7	6.28	13.6	4.57
%A (A, Ad)	55.0	22.46	43.0	25.06	52.3	19.70	54.6	16.91
H (H, Hd)	1.9	2.49	1.8	1.64	4.2	2.27	4.2	3.01
%H (H, Hd)	10.6	12.36	12.0	12.92	13.1	5.59	16.6	10.21
Content range	5.0	1.98	5.0	2.24	7.9	3.54	7.3	1.25
P	2.9	1.83	2.3	1.87	4.8	1.63	5.0	1.64
%P	18.4	11.12	15.6	13.95	19.0	10.84	20.9	9.41
O	2.8	4.86	1.8	2.71	3.6	2.57	2.8	1.92
%O	10.6	4.80	7.0	5.61	12.1	8.24	10.2	6.65

* Unless otherwise indicated, percentages are based on total R.
† %F+=F+/F.
‡ %M+=M+/M.

the mean number of each type of response? Second, there is the question of age at which the various types of responses tend to appear. That is, do certain types of responses appear earlier in one sex than in the other sex? These are two quite distinct questions, and there is no reason to suppose that the answers to them are necessarily related. It seems possible that sex differences might not appear in terms of means for the various determinants because those subjects who give a certain type of response may utilize it a disproportionate number of times. At the same time, sex differences might appear in the age at which the particular type of response occurs. For example, *if* boys tend to utilize M responses earlier than girls as Paulsen claims, it is possible that the girls who used M responses in the present study gave more of these responses and thus raised the mean number of M responses for girls.

Table 11 shows the percentage of boys and girls giving movement, color, and chiaroscuro responses. Also included in

TABLE 11.—SEX DIFFERENCES IN PERCENTAGE OF CHILDREN GIVING MOVEMENT, COLOR, AND CHIAROSCURO RESPONSES

Investigator...	*Ford*				*Paulsen*		*Stavrianos*					
Age..........	*3 to 6*		*6 to 8*		*6 to 7*		*5 to 7*		*7 to 9*		*9 to 11*	
Sex..........	*Boys*	*Girls*	*Boys*	*Girls*	*Boys*	*Girls*	*Boys*	*Girls*	*Boys*	*Girls*	*Boys*	*Girls*
Subjects......	*36*	*41*	*21*	*25*	*20*	*20*	*35*	*47*	*27*	*24*	*20*	*20*
DETERMINANT												
M	25	14	81	68	57	38	0	35	41	54	60	60
FM	64	49	95	89								
m	6	5	5	0								
No M, FM, m..	33	49	0	1								
FC	33	51	57	53	26	34	55	65	56	54	55	60
CF	32	51	67	52	49	57	55	20	41	63	35	45
C	19	22	52	28	38	51	15	30	4	29	15	5
Cn	35	35	0	0								
No FC, CF, C...	39	20	24	20			30	20	33	4	25	30
K	17	12	43	52								

this table are comparable data from the studies of Paulsen and Stavrianos. There is little agreement between the data of the three studies. Part of this difference may be due to the fact that the age groups are somewhat different in each study. Another factor contributing to the difference may be the character of the individual samples. As far as can be judged from the brief description of subjects given by Paulsen and Stavrianos, it would seem that their groups were composed of average children, while the subjects in the present study were superior both in intelligence and in socio-economic status. Neither of these factors, however, can explain completely the diversity of results reported in Table 11. The writer suspects that the major factor underlying the differences is the scoring of the records. As has been pointed out previously, it is extremely difficult to make some of the finer distinctions in determinants, especially in color responses, when the subjects are young children.

In the present study the preschool boys tended to utilize movement (both M and FM) responses earlier than the preschool girls. This is indicated in two ways. Nearly half of the preschool girls, in contrast to one third of the preschool boys, gave no movement responses; one fourth of the preschool boys, compared to 14 per cent of the preschool girls, gave at least one M response; and 64 per cent of the preschool boys, compared to 49 per cent of the preschool girls, gave at least one FM response.* These differences are not large enough to rule out the chance that they may be attributes of the particular sample and not characteristics of the population of young children. In the older group these sex differences tend to disappear except that the proportion of boys is still greater than the proportion of girls utilizing at least one M response (*CR* 1.04). Disregarding the differences in the percentage of children giving at least one M response and considering only the sex differences, Paulsen's data in respect to the earlier appearance of M responses in boys than in girls are in agreement with the findings of this investigation (*CR* 1.73, calculated from Paulsen's data). Although Stavrianos reports a reverse relationship for her youngest group, it is interesting to find that in her 7- to 9-year-old group the direction of the sex difference agrees with the findings of Paulsen's study and the present study (*CR* 0.94, calculated from Stavrianos' data).

In the present study more than one third of the preschool boys, in contrast to one fifth of the preschool girls, gave no color (C, CF, and FC) responses (*CR* 1.85). A larger proportion of preschool girls than preschool boys gave FC and CF responses (*CR* 1.63 and 1.72 respectively), but there is little difference between the proportions of preschool boys and girls who gave C responses. In the older group the proportions of boys and girls giving FC responses are similar, but more boys than girls gave CF and C responses (*CR* 1.05 and 1.70 respectively). About equal proportions of boys and girls gave no color responses. Disregarding the actual proportions of children using the various color determinants, there is agreement among the three studies in the direction of the sex difference. That is, in each study girls appear to utilize all the color determinants

* *CR* 1.45, 1.22, and 1.39 respectively.

earlier than boys. Although the sex differences in color determinants are not large enough to rule out the chance that they may be attributed to the particular sample, the differences are greater than those reported by Paulsen and Stavrianos.

The evidence in the present study supports the claim made by previous investigators that young children, especially preschool children, give fewer shading (K) responses. While the proportions of children giving K responses are markedly larger in the older group than in the preschool group, there is relatively little difference between the boys and girls in either group.

Of the three distinct hypotheses in respect to sex differences, two are supported in part and one is not supported by the evidence in the present study. The number of whole and detail responses are similar for boys and girls. This finding does not agree with those of Paulsen and Stavrianos, who claim that boys tend to give more whole and girls more detail responses. Although almost no sex differences appear between the means of movement and color responses, they do occur when the responses are analyzed in terms of percentage of children utilizing them. Boys tend to utilize movement responses sooner than girls, whereas girls tend to utilize color responses sooner than boys. These two findings agree with those reported by Paulsen and Stavrianos except that the latter investigator reported the earlier appearance of M responses in the records of girls than in the records of boys.

X. RELIABILITIES OF THE TEST DETERMINANTS

No previous attempt has been made to study the reliability of the Rorschach Test at the preschool level. This is due in part to the fact that the test has only recently been used with preschool children and in part to the fact that the diagnostic significance of the test depends upon the relationships between the various determinants rather than upon the incidence of these determinants. Many Rorschach workers claim that analysis of the consistency of isolated determinants is meaningless because these determinants have meaning only in relation to the other variables in an individual record. Though it is true that in the Rorschach Test, to a greater extent than in most other tests, the interrelationships rather than the incidence of determinants are of paramount importance, the writer agrees with Hertz (68) that a study of the consistency of the parts contributes some evidence on the consistency of the whole.

In order to study the reliability of the test at the preschool level, 55 of the preschool children in this study were given a second test approximately one month after their first test. Originally it was planned to retest all the preschool children. This plan had to be modified later because of lack of time. As far as could be determined, no selective factor which could influence reliability entered into the selection of the 55 cases retested. The basis for the selection of retest cases was entirely dependent upon the time of the examiner and the availability of the subjects. Some of the original subjects had been withdrawn from school and some were absent during the time when retests were given. The retest group was composed of 20 3-year-olds, 22 4-year-olds, and 13 5-year-olds.

Pearson product-moment correlation coefficients were calculated for the various test-retest determinants. These are presented in Table 12 together with their relative deviates.* The reliabilities of the determinants are all positive and range from +.38 to +.86. Since each of the k_r values in the table is greater than 2.58, and since the probability that a deviate of this magnitude will be exceeded is 0.0099, it may be concluded that each coefficient indicates a significant relationship between

* $k_r = r\sqrt{N-1}$ (134, pp. 155–56).

TABLE 12.—TEST-RETEST RELIABILITIES OF RORSCHACH DETERMINANTS AT THE PRESCHOOL LEVEL

DETERMINANT	COEFFICIENT (N=55)	RELATIVE DEVIATE (k_r)
R	+.76	5.59
Obj	+.55	4.04
OL	+.63	4.63
W (W, DW, WS)	+.75	5.51
D	+.60	4.41
Dr	+.72	5.29
%W (W, DW, WS)*	+.72	5.29
%D	+.51	3.75
%Dr	+.66	4.85
F	+.72	5.29
F+	+.70	5.15
M (M, FM, m)	+.86	6.32
M+ (M, FM, m)	+.78	5.73
C, CF, FC	+.68	5.00
%F	+.76	5.59
%F+†	+.49	3.60
%M (M, FM, m)	+.85	6.25
%M+ (M, FM, m)‡	+.52	3.82
%C, CF, FC	+.69	5.07
C-sum	+.71	5.22
A (A, Ad)	+.62	4.56
%A (A, Ad)	+.76	5.59
Content range	+.67	4.92
P	+.65	4.78
%P	+.66	4.85
O	+.72	5.29
%O	+.70	5.15
%O+§	+.38	2.79

* Unless otherwise indicated, percentages are based on total R.
† %F+=F+/F.
‡ %M+=M+/M.
§ %O+=O+/O.

the test and retest determinant. In other words, each relationship is above the 1 per cent level of significance. When one considers that these reliabilities are based on the test results of preschool children, it is even more surprising to find such high coefficients, because the reliabilities of other tests at the preschool level are usually considerably lower than the reliabilities of these same tests when used with older subjects. In addition, test-retest reliabilities are, in general, lower than comparable reliabilities calculated by the odd-even method and adjusted according to the Spearman-Brown correction.

In order to compare the reliabilities of Rorschach determinants at the preschool level with the reported reliabilities of these determinants at older age levels, the odd-even coefficients were calculated for both the test and the retest. Since in the literature reliabilities are reported only in terms of percentage of occurrence, this practice is followed in the odd-even correlations in the present study. It will be noted that certain coefficients are lacking in Table 13. No reliabilities are reported for %Dr, %M, %C, C-sum, %O, or %P, because the absence or low incidence of occurrence, when the test is divided into two parts, made a comparison meaningless. Furthermore, the definite tendency for some blots to suggest to young children certain types of responses makes the whole procedure of basing reliabilities on odd-even correlation coefficients questionable. One evidence of the validity of this conclusion is the low reliabilities of %W and %D when these coefficients are based on the odd-even method, in comparison with the relatively high reliabilities found when the test-retest method is used. A further illustration of the lack of balance between the split halves of the test is the fact that there are three gray and two colored blots in the odd half as compared with two gray and three colored blots in the even half. The writer is inclined to question the real significance of the odd-even method of determining reliabilities in the case of many of the Rorschach determinants. Especially when the records of young children form the basis of analysis, the division of the test into two parts gives an inadequate sampling of many of the test determinants. This inadequacy, being basic to the material involved, cannot be com-

TABLE 13.—ODD-EVEN RELIABILITIES OF RORSCHACH DETERMINANTS AT THE PRESCHOOL LEVEL

	FIRST TEST (N=55)			RETEST (N=55)		
DETERMINANT	COEFFICIENT	k_r	CORRECTION*	COEFFICIENT	k_r	CORRECTION*
R	+.76	5.59	+.86	+.75	5.51	+.86
Obj	+.84	6.17	+.91	+.75	5.51	+.86
OL	+.84	6.17	+.91	+.81	5.95	+.90
%W (W, DW, WS)	+.15	1.10	+.26	+.34	2.50	+.51
%D	+.01	0.07	+.02	+.19	1.40	+.32
%F	+.63	4.63	+.77	+.66	4.85	+.82
%F+	+.49	3.60	+.66	+.55	4.04	+.71
%A	+.47	3.45	+.64	+.37	2.72	+.54

* Spearman-Brown formula: $r_{12} = \frac{2r}{1+r}$

pensated for by any statistical device to correct for length of the test.

There are, however, some Rorschach determinants that can be studied as adequately by one reliability method as by the other. These determinants are R, Obj, OL, %F, %F+, and to a limited extent %A. The reliability coefficients of these determinants range from +.47 to +.84 on the first test and from +.37 to +.75 on the retest. Each is above the 1 per cent level of significance and, as has generally been indicated in studies of reliability methods, the magnitude of each coefficient when corrected by the Spearman-Brown formula exceeds the comparable test-retest reliability coefficient. There is one exception. The test-retest coefficient is greater than either of the odd-even coefficients in the case of %A. Here again one is inclined to suspect that the blots which are especially apt to stimulate animal responses are not evenly divided between the split halves.

A comparison of the reliabilities of various Rorschach determinants reported by other investigators and those found in the present study is presented in Table 14. Some of the reliabilities reported by Hertz (58) and some of those reported in this in-

TABLE 14.—COMPARISON OF REPORTED RORSCHACH RELIABILITIES WITH THOSE FOUND IN THE PRESENT STUDY*

Investigator	*Vernon*	*Hertz*	*Troup*	*Kerr*	*Ford*		
Subjects . . .	*90*	*100*	*20*	*30*	*55*		
Age	*Adults*	*12½ to 16½*	*10 to 14*	*7 to 12*		*3 to 6*	
Method	*Split-half*	*Split-half*	*Retest*	*Retest*	*Split-half†*	*Split-half ‡*	*Retest*
DETERMINANT							
R	+.91	+.890			+.86	+.86	+.76
Obj		+.864			+.91	+.86	+.55
%W	+.74	+.835	+.82	+.74	+.26	+.51	+.72
%D		+.750			+.02	+.32	+.51
%F		+.807			+.77	+.82	+.76
%F+	+.33	+.730			+.66	+.71	+.49
%M	+.62	+.745	+.79	+.52			+.85
%C	+.34	+.810					+.69
C-sum		+.763					+.71
%A	+.48	+.829	+.56	+.52	+.64	+.54	+.76
%O	+.60						+.70
%O+		+.911					+.38
%P	+.64	+.666	+.77	+.61			+.66

* Each split-half coefficient corrected by Spearman-Brown formula. Retest intervals: Troup, 6 months; Kerr, 1 year; Ford, 1 month.

† First test.

‡ Retest.

vestigation are not included in the table because of the lack of other comparable data. Analysis of the data in Table 14 indicates that the reliabilities reported by Hertz are, in general, higher than those reported by the other investigators. Hertz ascribes the difference between her coefficients and those reported by Vernon to her refinement of procedure and scoring. The fact that Hertz's coefficients are higher than those reported by Troup and Kerr may be due in part to the methods used—split-half versus test-retest—and in part to the fact that the subjects in the latter studies were younger than those in Hertz's study.

With the exception of %W, %D, and %A, the coefficients reported by Hertz are quite comparable to those found by the split-half method in the present study. This seems to indicate that for these determinants at least, age is not a factor in lowering the reliabilities. The fact that the test-retest coefficients in the present study are lower for these determinants would, therefore, seem to result more from method than from age. For the remaining determinants, with two exceptions, the test-retest coefficients are consistently a little lower than those reported by Hertz. The coefficient for %M is somewhat higher and for %O+ considerably lower than those reported by Hertz. In general, Kerr's coefficients tend to agree with Vernon's in being lower than those found in the other studies. This is not surprising since the interval between tests in Kerr's study was one year.

In summary it may be said that the reliability coefficients reported in the present study, while not high, are higher than those reported by Vernon and Kerr. They are comparable to those reported by Troup. In most cases the split-half coefficients are comparable to those reported by Hertz, while the test-retest reliabilities tend to be somewhat lower. The evidence of this investigation suggests that with further refinement of procedure and scoring, the reliabilities of the various test determinants may be expected to approximate those of other standard tests for young children. Even at the present time, under the conditions set up in this study, the reliabilities of most of the determinants are fairly satisfactory, especially when one considers that the interpretation of test results does not depend upon any one determinant but upon the balance and interrelationship between determinants.

XI. VALIDITY OF THE DETERMINANTS OF INTELLIGENCE

Rorschach's claims concerning the relationship between various test determinants and intelligence are presented in Table 1 (Chapter II). From this table it is evident that Rorschach considers W, M, and %F+ to be directly related to intelligence, %A inversely related, and %O and C to increase as the intellectual level increases but also to increase as the intellectual level decreases. In other words, %O and C may be expected to be greater in both very superior and feebleminded subjects than in subjects of average intelligence. Vernon's study (145) does not support the above claims. However, the findings presented by Hertz (57) and Beck (7), which are given in Table 2 (Chapter II), are in general agreement with Rorschach's claims, although the correlations reported, except possibly in the case of %F+, are low.

When this study was undertaken, only one attempt had been made to study the relationship between intelligence and Rorschach determinants given by young children. Paulsen (112) found no relationship between intelligence and R, W, and D, but she claims that there is a marked difference between bright and dull children in the quality of W responses. In her study M, %F+, FC, K, P, S, A, and H responses were directly related to intelligence, and %F was inversely related. Less gifted children tended to give more C responses than did more gifted children, but no relationship appeared between CF responses and intellectual level. Paulsen concludes that although these trends are quite apparent, the wide individual differences make it impossible to use any one or two factors predictively. No figures are given to substantiate the above claims.

Rorschach does not discuss the possible effect of age on the relationship between the various determinants and intelligence. Paulsen's findings and the experience of the writer suggest that certain modifications may appear in the reported relationships of the test determinants when these determinants are based on the records of young children. To determine the relationship between mental age and the various test determinants, the subjects in the present study were divided into three groups

TABLE 15.—MEANS OF THE RORSCHACH DETERMINANTS IN RELATION TO MENTAL AGE

Mental age	*4-0 to 5-11*		*6-0 to 7-11*		*8-0 to 9-11*	
Subjects	*43*		*43*		*27*	
Average CA	*4-0*		*5-9*		*6-11*	
Average IQ	*123.6*		*122.0*		*127.7*	
DETERMINANT	MEAN	SD	MEAN	SD	MEAN	SD
R	15.9	6.01	19.2	6.98	29.2	10.36
Obj	22.1	9.41	28.2	9.30	44.0	15.09
OL	10.2	7.60	18.5	10.68	35.3	16.72
W (W, DW, WS)	5.3	1.82	5.6	1.98	6.2	3.73
D	8.7	4.97	11.1	5.34	18.3	6.85
Dr	0.9	1.19	1.5	1.96	3.4	4.28
Do	0.7	1.11	0.6	0.89	0.8	1.13
DS	0.4	0.56	0.4	0.68	0.6	0.72
%W (W, DW, WS)*	38.1	18.13	32.4	14.63	23.1	12.79
%D	51.4	16.89	56.7	13.53	62.3	9.61
%Dr	4.7	6.44	6.4	7.12	9.6	7.44
%Do	4.1	5.91	2.5	4.31	2.9	4.27
%DS	2.1	3.32	2.0	4.08	2.0	2.46
F	13.4	5.37	13.9	5.79	21.2	9.25
F+	6.0	3.45	8.6	3.71	14.9	6.36
M (M, FM, m)	0.9	1.06	2.8	2.18	5.7	2.61
M+ (M, FM, m)	0.7	0.91	2.2	1.60	4.0	3.32
C, CF, FC	1.4	1.64	2.3	1.69	2.1	2.48
%F	84.8	12.41	71.9	12.13	73.0	14.75
%F+†	44.0	21.07	64.3	18.49	70.2	11.43
%M (M, FM, m)	5.6	6.81	14.9	11.71	17.8	12.98
%M+ (M, FM, m)‡	35.1	32.64	65.0	39.10	73.0	32.09
%C, CF, FC	8.8	11.09	11.6	7.82	7.3	6.58
C-sum	1.2	1.37	2.2	1.92	2.2	2.51
A (A, Ad)	7.6	4.00	9.7	3.80	15.4	6.85
%A (A, Ad)	49.5	26.10	51.5	15.94	54.9	16.46
H (H, Hd)	1.6	1.93	2.5	2.56	4.4	3.05
%H (H, Hd)	10.6	10.15	11.2	11.04	16.2	9.21
Content range	5.1	2.43	7.0	2.52	9.3	3.48
P	1.9	1.59	4.2	1.62	5.2	1.71
%P	13.3	11.29	24.0	12.41	19.7	9.57
O	1.1	1.46	1.9	1.76	3.3	2.13
%O	5.6	7.25	9.2	8.53	11.1	6.68
%O+§	26.5	37.88	46.5	40.75	85.0	25.01

* Unless otherwise indicated, percentages are based on total R.
† %F+=F+/F.
‡ %M+=M+/M.
§ %O+=O+/O.

on the basis of mental age as indicated by Form L of the Stanford-Binet test. Forty-three of the children had mental ages between 4 years and 5 years 11 months, 43 between 6 years and 7 years 11 months, and 27 between 8 years and 9 years 11 months. Five subjects with mental ages below 4 years and 5 subjects with mental ages above 10 years were not included in

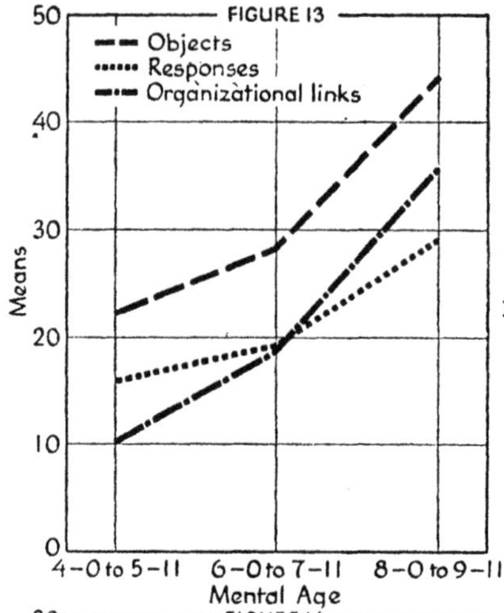

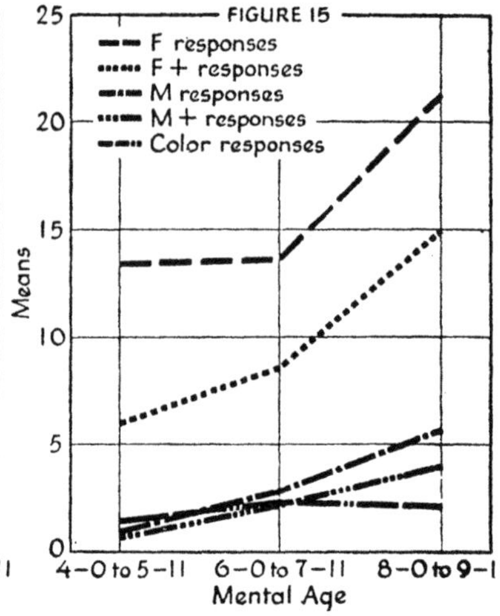

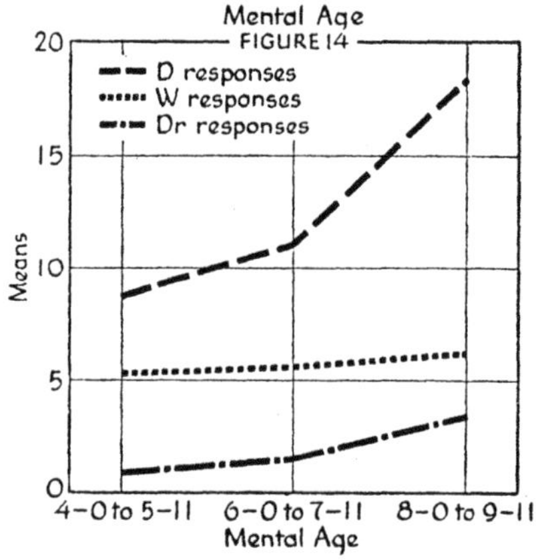

Figure 13.—Mean Number of Responses, Objects, and Organizational Links in Relation to Mental Age. *Figure 14.*—Manner of Apperception in Relation to Mental Age (Mean Number of W, D, and Dr Responses). *Figure 15.*—Quality of Response in Relation to Mental Age (Mean Number of F, F+, M, M+, and Color Responses).

this comparison. The means of the Rorschach determinants at the various intellectual levels are presented in Table 15.

It is evident from Table 15 and Figure 13 that R and Obj increase with increasing mental age. Although Rorschach and Paulsen reported no relationship between R and intelligence, it is not surprising that such a relationship appears in the present study. The young children in this study are still within the age range where language is developing rapidly, whereas Rorschach's subjects were adults with already well-developed ability to use language, and Paulsen's subjects included only one age group. The Pearson product-moment correlation between mental age and R is +.634 and between mental age and Obj +.620 (k_r=7.00 and 7.51 respectively). The fact that Beck

(7) found no relationship between R and mental age ($r = -.012 \pm .08$) in his feebleminded group suggests that the relationship found in this study is probably a function of chronological age as well as mental age and that the reported relationship is valid only in the case of young children who are not mentally retarded.

Table 15 and Figure 14 indicate that there is little relationship between mental age and each of the determinants descriptive of the mode of response. Thus Rorschach's claim that W is indicative of the intellectual level of the subject is not substantiated when the test is used with young children, since the correlation between mental age and W is +.103 $k_r = 1.14$). This is not in agreement with Beck's finding of a relatively high correlation between W and mental age ($r = +.474 \pm .06$). It is quite possible that the tendency of very young children to give poor quality W and DW responses, thus raising the number of W responses at the early levels, is a factor contributing to the low relationship between W and mental age when the test is used with young children. Figures 14 and 16 indicate that the increase in R with increasing mental age is paralleled by a gradual increase in D and Dr responses both in terms of number of these responses and in terms of percentage of occurrence. This increase, however, is too gradual to be useful as a basis for the prediction of mental level. Beck also found no relationship between Dr and mental age. In terms of percentage of total R, W responses given by young children decrease slightly with increasing mental age. Irrespective of mental age, the young children in this study gave few DS and Do responses as indicated by the data in Table 15. The fact that Do responses are present in the records of some of the children in this study does not substantiate Rorschach's claim that Do responses appear only in records of feebleminded subjects or of subjects who are in depressive or anxiety states. The finding in the present study is in agreement with Beck, who reported little relationship between Do and mental age ($r = -.069 \pm .08$).

Table 15 and Figures 15 and 17 indicate that F+, M, and M+ responses in terms both of averages and of percentages increase with increasing mental age. Thus Rorschach's claim that %F+ and M are indicative of the mental level of the subject is substantiated by the evidence in this investigation. The correlations between M and %F+ and mental age are +.581

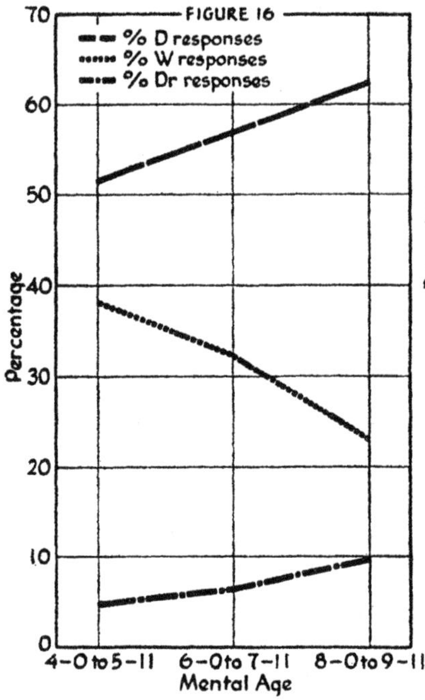

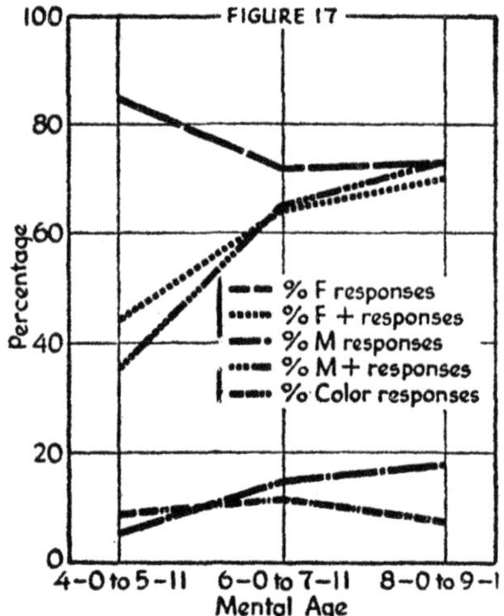

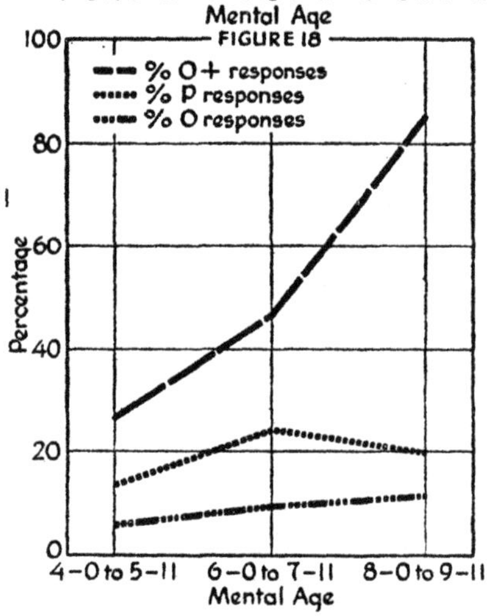

Figure 16.—MANNER OF APPERCEPTION IN RELATION TO MENTAL AGE (PERCENTAGE OF W, D, AND DR RESPONSES). *Figure 17.*—QUALITY OF RESPONSE IN RELATION TO MENTAL AGE (PERCENTAGE OF F, F+, M, M+, AND COLOR RESPONSES). *Figure 18.*—PERCENTAGE OF P, O, AND O+ RESPONSES IN RELATION TO MENTAL AGE.

and +.612 respectively (k_r=6.42 and 6.76 respectively). In the case of %F+ the correlation with mental age is similar to that reported by Beck (r=+.640±.051), but the correlation between M and mental age in this study is higher than in Beck's study (r=+.256±.079). Since Rorschach maintained that M is indicative of creativity, it is not surprising to find a closer relationship between M and mental age in this study, where the subjects range from average to very superior. Beck's subjects, being feebleminded, would be expected to be quite restricted in the range of their creativity.

The relationship between movement responses and mental

age is shown even more clearly in Table 16, where movement responses are broken down into M, FM, and m responses as suggested by Klopfer. Because of the sex differences in the occurrence of movement, color, and chiaroscuro responses reported in Chapter IX, the percentages of boys and girls utilizing these determinants were calculated separately. The few m responses present in the records in this study show no relationship to mental age. As indicated in Table 16 and Figure 19, the percentage of children using M and FM increases markedly with increasing mental age, but, as in the case of chronological age, there is a consistent tendency for more boys than girls, at each mental age level, to utilize these responses.

TABLE 16.—PERCENTAGE OF BOYS AND GIRLS GIVING MOVEMENT, COLOR, AND CHIAROSCURO RESPONSES IN RELATION TO MENTAL AGE

Mental age	*4-0 to 5-11*			*6-0 to 7-11*			*8-0 to 9-11*		
Sex	*Boys*	*Girls*	*Both*	*Boys*	*Girls*	*Both*	*Boys*	*Girls*	*Both*
Subjects	*22*	*21*	*43*	*20*	*23*	*43*	*10*	*17*	*27*
DETERMINANT									
M	18	5	12	45	43	44	90	65	74
FM	55	43	49	85	74	79	100	88	93
m	0	0	0	10	9	9	10	0	4
No M, FM, m	45	57	51	5	26	16	0	6	4
FC	23	48	35	60	61	60	60	41	48
CF	32	48	40	45	52	49	70	59	63
C	5	19	12	45	35	40	50	24	33
Cn	27	38	33	25	13	19	0	0	0
No FC, CF, C, Cn	36	24	30	15	9	12	20	24	22
K	9	14	12	45	26	35	20	47	37

Color responses, in terms of averages, show little relationship to mental age. The correlation between C-sum and mental age is, however, $+.252$ ($k_r = 2.78$), indicating a slight relationship between color responses and mental age. Since Beck calculated the correlation between the number of color responses and mental age, his finding of no relationship between color responses and mental age ($r = +.012 \pm .08$) is not entirely comparable to the correlation in the present study.

When the percentage of boys and girls using the various color responses is calculated (see Table 16 and Figure 20), it is interesting to note that more girls than boys in the lowest mental age group utilize each of the color determinants, that the sex difference in the intermediate group is less marked, and that in the highest mental age group more boys than girls use each of

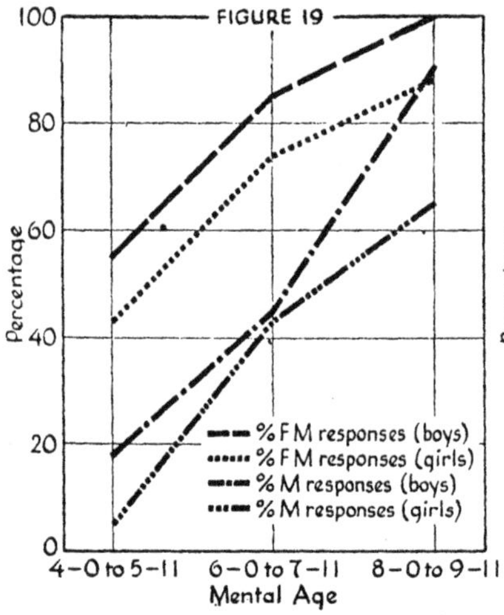

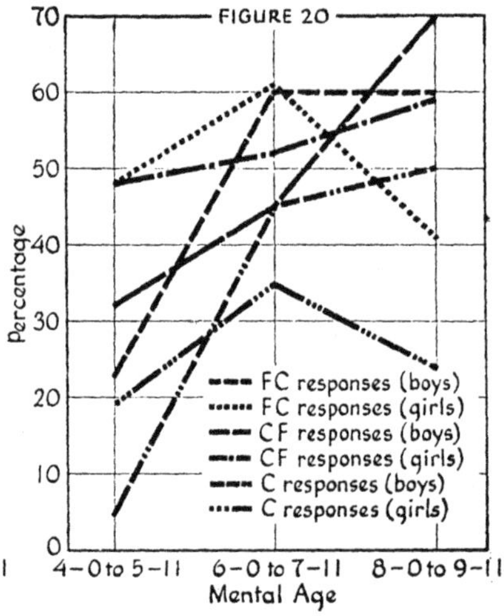

Figure 19.—PERCENTAGE OF BOYS AND GIRLS USING M AND FM RESPONSES IN RELATION TO MENTAL AGE. *Figure 20.*—PERCENTAGE OF BOYS AND GIRLS USING FC, CF, AND COLOR RESPONSES IN RELATION TO MENTAL AGE.

the determinants. Cn, the most elementary form of color response, decreases with increasing mental age. It is not utilized by any child in the highest mental age group. The percentage of boys and girls giving CF responses and the percentage of boys giving C responses increase with increasing mental age, whereas the percentages of girls giving C responses and FC responses increase between the lowest and the intermediate mental age groups but decrease in the highest mental age group. The percentage of boys giving FC responses increases between the lowest and intermediate mental age group but is identical for the intermediate and highest mental age groups. If FC is, as claimed by Rorschach, indicative of "adaptive affective responsiveness," an increase in FC responses would be expected in the highest mental age group. Since the children in this group were on the average 6 years 11 months old, they were at the age when they were experiencing their first formal schooling. It is interesting to speculate on the possible effect of this experience in temporarily lowering their ability to make stable emotional adaptation. On the basis of the evidence of this study, this speculation is worth further investigation.

As indicated in Table 16, the percentage of boys using K responses increases between the first two groups but decreases in the highest mental age group. The girls show a marked increase in K responses with increasing mental age. Although the interpretation of the K determinant, like all other Rorschach determinants, depends upon its relation to the other determinants, in general K responses are indicative of insecurity. If this interpretation is valid, then the finding of an increase of K responses with both increasing mental age and increasing chronological age is extremely suggestive for further investigation. Means for the various movement, color, and K determinants in relation to mental age are given in Table 17.

TABLE 17.—MEANS FOR M, FM, m, FC, CF, C, Cn, AND K RESPONSES IN RELATION TO MENTAL AGE

Mental age	*4-0 to 5-11*	*6-0 to 7-11*	*8-0 to 9-11*
Subjects	*43*	*43*	*27*
DETERMINANT			
M	0.1	0.7	2.1
FM	0.7	2.1	2.9
m	0	0.1	0
FC	0.6	0.8	0.6
CF	0.6	0.7	1.2
C	0.2	0.7	0.4
Cn	0.7	0.2	0
K	0.2	0.4	0.7

Table 15 indicates that the number of A and H responses increases slightly with increasing mental age. When A and H responses are calculated in terms of percentage of total R, there is a slight increase in %H with increasing mental age, but %A remains relatively constant in relation to mental age. Rorschach's claim that %A is inversely related to mental level is not substantiated by the evidence here, since the correlation between %A and mental age is +.070 (k_r=0.77). The finding in the present study is, however, in agreement with that reported by Beck (7). He found a correlation of +.156±.079 between %A and mental age. The only other relationship between content of the response and mental age is indicated by the tendency of the content range to increase gradually with increasing mental age.

As indicated in Table 15, there is a slight tendency for P and O responses to increase with increasing mental age. When these responses are calculated in terms of percentage of total R (see Figure 18), %O increases with increasing mental age, whereas

%P appears to be greater for the intermediate mental age group than for the other two groups. It must be remembered that both P and O responses in this study are scored on the basis of P and O responses in adolescents and adults, since no norms are available for these responses in young children.

When original responses based on good form (O+) are calculated in terms of percentage of O responses, there is a marked increase in %O+ with increasing mental age. The correlation between %O+ and mental age is +.580 (k_r=6.41). Beck's finding of a negative relationship between %O and mental age ($r=-.391\pm.068$) is not as contradictory as it appears to be. According to Rorschach, %O is highest for individuals of very superior intelligence, decreases for average individuals, and increases again in the records of feebleminded subjects. Rorschach claimed also that O responses at the higher mental levels are predominantly based on good form (O+), while those at the feebleminded level are predominantly based on poor form (O—). Because of the inadequacies of norms for O+ and O— at the time his study was made, Beck did not attempt to separate O+ and O—. Had he been able to do this, the correlation between %O+ and mental age probably would have exceeded in magnitude the correlation between %O and mental age, but the direction of the relationship would have remained unchanged. Thus Rorschach's claim concerning the relationship between O responses and intellectual level is supported by the findings of this study and Beck's.

Early experimentation with Rorschach records of very young children showed considerable individual variation in the ability of young children to relate logically the various parts of their responses. For example, one child might give the response "men" to the black portions of card III. Another child of the same age might amplify his similar response by naming one or two parts of the men, such as legs, head, or arms. The response of a third child, "men dancing with baskets," although based on similar descriptions of similar forms, indicates markedly superior ability to organize elements into a creative, logical interpretation. Since the ability to interpret wholes has been utilized in other tests as a measure of mental level, it seemed possible that such an analysis applied to Rorschach records of young children might help to differentiate mental levels. As pointed out previously, OL responses were found to increase with increasing chronological age but showed an even more marked increase with increasing mental age. The correlation between OL and mental age is +.684 (k_r=7.56), which is comparable to the correlations between mental age and R, Obj, M, and %F+ and is somewhat higher than the correlation between mental age and %O+. It would seem, therefore, that OL is as closely related to intelligence as these other determinants when the test is used with young children.

Early in this chapter the hypothesis was advanced that the determinants which Rorschach claimed were indicative of intellectual level might need some modification when the test is applied to young children. To test this hypothesis further, the subjects in the present study were divided into three groups—average, superior, and very superior—on the basis of IQ on Form L of the Stanford-Binet. The means of the various determinants in relation to IQ are presented in Tables 18 and 19. Although in most cases the means increase with increasing intellectual level, it is evident that the variation within a group is greater than the variation between groups. The incidence according to Rorschach of W, M, C, %F+, %A, and %O for average, superior and very superior subjects is given in Table 1 (Chapter II). A comparison of the expected incidence and the actual means found in this study indicates clearly that Rorschach norms for comparable mental levels bear almost no relationship to the findings of this investigation. In other words, although with few exceptions the relationships between various

TABLE 18.—MEANS FOR VARIOUS RORSCHACH DETERMINANTS IN RELATION TO IQ

IQ	*90 to 109*		*110 to 129*		*130 to 159*	
Subjects	*18*		*62*		*43*	
Average CA	*5-7*		*5-5*		*5-2*	
Average MA	*5-8*		*6-7*		*7-3*	
DETERMINANT	MEAN	SD	MEAN	SD	MEAN	SD
R	19.2	7.19	19.6	10.27	22.5	8.36
Obj	25.3	12.21	29.6	16.06	32.5	15.01
OL	12.8	12.14	19.8	16.70	21.7	15.82
W	5.1	1.83	5.6	2.42	5.6	2.64
M	1.5	1.42	2.8	3.33	2.7	2.41
%F+	50.4	17.44	55.7	18.00	64.8	20.97
C-sum	1.6	1.82	1.7	1.83	2.1	2.07
%A	46.3	27.51	53.7	19.99	48.5	19.49
%O	5.8	6.36	7.8	8.24	10.2	7.84
%O+	38.3	39.24	38.9	41.12	66.0	40.94

TABLE 19.—MEANS FOR M, FM, m, FC, CF, C, Cn, AND K RESPONSES IN RELATION TO IQ

IQ	*90 to 109*	*110 to 129*	*130 to 159*
Subjects	*18*	*62*	*43*
DETERMINANT			
M	0.1	0.9	0.9
FM	0.9	1.9	1.8
m	0	0.1	0.2
FC	0.5	0.8	0.9
CF	0.6	0.8	0.8
C	0.5	0.3	0.6
Cn	0.2	0.3	0.5
K	0.3	0.3	0.6

determinants and mental level are substantiated in terms of mental age, they are not substantiated in terms of IQ.

This fact is further illustrated in the comparison of the relationships between the various determinants and mental age and IQ. The correlations in Table 20 indicate that R, Obj, M, %F+, %O+, and OL are fairly closely related to mental age, and that C-sum is less closely but still positively related. The relationship between IQ and R, Obj, M, %F+, %O+, and OL is considerably less marked, and C-sum shows almost no relation to IQ. The differences between the relationship of the various determinants to MA and IQ may be ascribed in part to the fact that the various determinants have been shown previously to vary with chronological as well as mental age. In this connection it is important to note that the average CA decreases with increase in IQ. The very superior children are, therefore, chronologically somewhat less mature than the

TABLE 20.—CORRELATIONS BETWEEN VARIOUS RORSCHACH DETERMINANTS AND MA AND IQ*

	MA		IQ	
DETERMINANT	r	k_r	r	k_r
R	+.634	7.00	+.194	2.14
Obj	+.680	7.51	+.235	2.60
OL	+.684	7.56	+.223	2.46
W	+.103	1.14	−.048	0.53
M	+.581	6.42	+.186	2.05
%F+	+.612	6.76	+.306	3.38
C-sum	+.252	2.78	+.050	0.55
%A	+.070	0.77	−.019	0.21
%O+	+.580	6.41	+.276	3.05

* $N=123$.

less gifted groups. This may well be a factor in lowering the relationship between the various determinants and IQ. The fact that there is still a difference attributable to intelligence as such is more important than the correlations in Table 20 would seem to indicate, since at the very young age level the handicap of even a month or two is of importance. This fact makes it increasingly evident that adequate norms for young children must be established before the Rorschach Test can be used to maximum advantage with young children. It is also evident that these norms must be established for each year level rather than for preschool children as a group.

Although Table 20 summarizes the findings of this chapter concerning the relationship between the various determinants and intellectual level, it may well be pointed out that the correlations between M, %F+, %A, and %O+ and intelligence, while slightly smaller in magnitude, are quite comparable to those reported by Hertz (see Table 2, Chapter II). Hertz reports a correlation of +.209 between C-sum and IQ, but no relationship was found between these two variables in the present study. The main discrepancy between the correlations reported by Hertz and those found here occurs in W responses. Hertz's correlation is +.241 as compared with −.048 in the present study. Although Paulsen gives no figures to substantiate her statement, she also finds no relationship between W and IQ. The other relationships reported by Paulsen are, with two exceptions, in general agreement with those reported in the present study. She found no relationship between R and intellectual level. In addition, she reports that less gifted children give more C responses. The present study, however, found that C responses increase slightly with increasing mental level.

XII. VALIDITY OF SOME OF THE DETERMINANTS OF PERSONALITY

One of the chief advantages of the Rorschach Test as a measure of the total personality structure of an individual is the presence of many interrelationships between the test determinants. Although these many, and often complicated, interrelationships serve as a check on the diagnosis of the psychological functioning of an individual, they complicate the problem of testing the hypotheses on which they are based. It was pointed out in the preceding chapter that no one determinant is the basis for predicting intellectual level. Even more complicated are the interrelationships on which personality dynamics are based. For this reason fewer attempts have been made to check the various hypotheses underlying the nonintellectual determinants. Whenever these attempts have been made, the results are unsatisfactory, chiefly because of two factors. First, taken out of their context the various determinants lose much of their meaning. Second, few outside tests are available which are themselves sufficiently reliable to serve as criteria for the validation of another test. This is especially true at the level of the very young child. As far as the writer knows, no attempt has been made to validate any of the hypotheses underlying the nonintellectual aspect of the Rorschach Test at the preschool level. Perhaps such an attempt is even now premature,

TABLE 21.—PERCENTAGE OF BOYS AND GIRLS SHOWING VARIOUS ERLEBNISTYPEN IN RELATION TO CHRONOLOGICAL AGE

*Age**		*3 years*	*4 years*	*5 years*	*6 years*	*7 years*
ERLEBNISTYP	SEX					
M>C-sum	Boys	46	42	64	64	70
	Girls	17	33	57	67	77
	Both	32	37	60	65	74
0 M, 0 C-sum	Boys	23	8	9	0	0
	Girls	17	27	7	8	0
	Both	20	19	8	4	0
M=C-sum	Boys	0	8	0	0	10
	Girls	0	0	7	0	8
	Both	0	4	4	0	9
M<C-sum	Boys	31	42	27	36	20
	Girls	67	40	29	25	15
	Both	48	41	28	31	17

* At 3 years, 13 boys and 12 girls; at 4 years, 12 boys and 15 girls; at 5 years, 11 boys and 14 girls; at 6 years, 11 boys and 12 girls; at 7 years, 10 boys and 13 girls.

since the many problems of scoring the Rorschach records of young children are just beginning to receive attention and since the solution of these problems is basic to interpretation. This chapter is written, therefore, with considerable hesitancy and with many reservations.

Essential to the understanding of how an individual functions is the determination of the relationship between his need to be outgoing and sociable and to seek stimulation and pleasure outside himself, and his need to be withdrawn and seclusive and to seek stimulation within himself. Rorschach claimed that no person is exclusively extroverted or introverted but that individuals tend to be extratensive or introversive to a greater or less degree. The relationship between this outer and inner stimulation is the core of Rorschach's theory of personality dynamics. *Erlebnistyp,* "experience type" or "experience balance," is represented in the Rorschach Test by the ratio M : C-sum. M responses, which according to Rorschach represent inner living and creativity, are a measure of introversive tendencies. C responses, representing sensitivity to stimuli from without, are a measure of extratensivity.

The balance between intrapsychic and extrapsychic living as indicated by the M : C-sum ratio was calculated for the subjects in this study. Table 21 and Figure 21 raise many questions. It would seem that the tendency toward introversive living increases directly with increasing chronological age between 3 and 7 years. More boys than girls show introversive tendencies at 3 years, and this relationship continues until sometime between 5 and 6 years, when it is reversed. At 3 years,

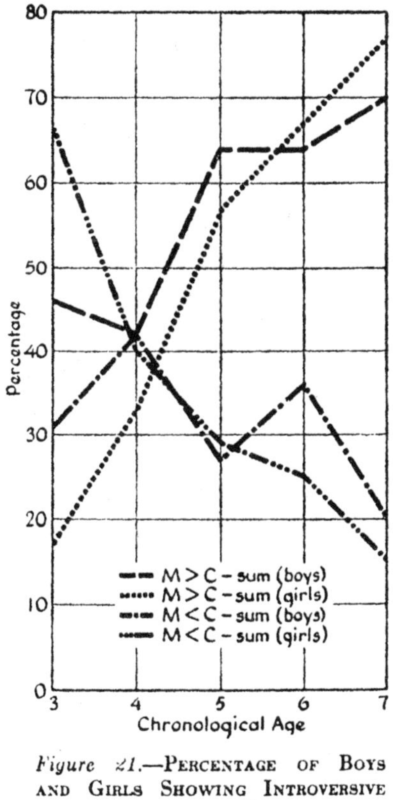

Figure 21.—PERCENTAGE OF BOYS AND GIRLS SHOWING INTROVERSIVE AND EXTRATENSIVE TENDENCIES IN RELATION TO CHRONOLOGICAL AGE

only 32 per cent of the total group show introversive tendencies, in contrast to 74 per cent at 7 years. At 3 years many more girls than boys show extratensive tendencies, between 4 and 5 years the sex difference disappears, and between 5 and 7 years slightly more boys than girls show extratensive tendencies. Whereas extratensive tendencies decrease directly with increasing chronological age in the case of the girls, the decrease is more irregular and less marked in the case of the boys. These findings are in agreement with those of Marston (99) but not with those of Paulsen, who made the only other study which reports the percentage of children showing introversive and extratensive tendencies as revealed by the Rorschach Test. Paulsen reports that 59 per cent of her group showed an extratensive balance and that only 29 per cent showed an introversive balance. No sex differences were apparent with the 7-year-olds. Paulsen's findings are more in line with what might be expected on the basis of our knowledge of young children.

The fact that the majority of the 5- to 7-year-old children in the present study show introversive tendencies may be, of course, a function of this particular sample of young children. In this connection it should be recalled that the subjects here are superior both in intelligence and in socio-economic status to average children of comparable age. Since creativity and richness of inner living are attributes of mental superiority, it is not too surprising to find these children endowed with more than average tendencies toward introversive living. On the other hand, the environment of most of these children is rich and challenging and, if utilized to its capacity, would tend to encourage more than average extratensive tendencies. If future studies verify the present findings, it would be interesting to study older children to determine when the impact of our extremely extratensive culture begins to impinge on the apparently rapidly developing inner living of young children, especially those of superior endowment.

In the above discussion it was assumed that the ratio M : C-sum does measure, as claimed by Rorschach and his followers, introversive and extratensive tendencies. The validity of this hypothesis is questioned by the findings of Vernon (145), Thornton and Guilford (138), and Line and Griffin (94). On the other hand, it is supported by Hertz (57) and Beck (7). In connection with the present investigation, Beck's finding that his feebleminded group showed a reliable tendency to be extratensive rather than introversive is significant. In the present study it was possible to secure teachers' ratings on the Marston Introversion-Extroversion Scale (99) for 30 of the preschool children. The correspondence between personality types as measured by the Marston scale and the Rorschach M : C-sum ratio is 60 per cent. This is relatively low and since Klopfer and Kelley (87) have contributed further refinement to the diagnosis of *Erlebnistyp*, it was possible to check the effect of the use of their supplementary formulas on this relationship between personality types as measured by the Marston and Rorschach scales. Unfortunately one of the formulas proved useless in this connection because it depends on the ratio (FM+m):(Fc+c+C′). That young children give very few m, Fc, c, and C′ responses has been generally agreed upon by all who have used the test with them.*

The second formula, based on the number of responses to cards VIII to X in relation to the total number of responses, is said to supplement the original Rorschach measure of *Erlebnistyp*. When this formula was used alone, it showed no more than a chance relationship (47 per cent) to the Marston scale. However, when the determination of *Erlebnistyp* was based on the M : C-sum ratio supplemented and checked by R(VIII–X):R, the correspondence between personality types as determined by these ratios and as measured by the Marston scale was increased to 73 per cent. This seems to support the claim made by many Rorschach workers that the supplementary measure improves the validity of diagnosis. This finding further illustrates the statement, repeated frequently in this study, that any one or two determinants taken out of context lose much of their original meaning.

Closely related to the question of the validity of the *Erlebnistyp* is the question of the reliability of this measure. Since no mention was made of this aspect of the Rorschach Test in the discussion on reliability (Chapter X), it is included here. The correspondence between personality types as measured by the M : C-sum ratio on first and second tests is 71 per cent, which compares favorably with Hertz's figure of 73 per cent

* Fc (responses based on form and texture), c (responses based on texture), and C′ (responses based on black and white) were not scored separately in this study. All responses based on the use of black and white, texture, and shading were designated K responses.

derived by the split-half method. The correlation between the R(VIII–X):R ratio based on first and second tests is +.375 (k_r=2.76). That the supplementation of the M: C-sum ratio with the R(VIII–X):R ratio improves the reliability of the determination of personality types is indicated by the increased percentage of agreement between first and second tests (82 per cent).

A second hypothesis underlying the nonintellectual aspect of the total personality picture as revealed by the Rorschach Test is concerned with color responses. As has been indicated earlier, Rorschach identified color responses with emotionality. That is, the number and balance between the various types of color responses is said to indicate the presence or absence of emotional adjustment. Here again the color determinants are to be interpreted not as isolated factors but in relation to the other determinants, especially M and %F+.

To test this hypothesis in the present study, the subjects were divided into three groups on the basis of their emotional adjustment as indicated by teachers' ratings on four items in the Olson Behavior Rating Scale. (Since the Olson scale is concerned primarily with the determination of problem tendencies, and since the degree of emotionality is not always directly related to these tendencies, it seemed more satisfactory to select from the scale those items which seemed to give an estimate of the subject's usual emotional approach to life situations.)* The subjects were then divided into three groups on the basis of emotional adjustment as indicated by the Rorschach Test. The relationship between teachers' ratings of emotional adjustment and emotional adjustment as measured by the Rorschach Test is shown by the contingency coefficient of .50. Inspection of the contingency table shows that the direction of the association is positive. Since only a threefold classification was used, the degree of association is probably underestimated. Thus the Rorschach Test seems to agree fairly closely with teachers' ratings in indicating the emotional status of the individual. This is in agreement with Hertz's (57) finding of r_t=+.66 between stable and unstable groups classed on the basis of the Rorschach Test and the Woodworth-Mathews total score. It is

* Items selected were: 25. Is he even tempered or moody? 29. How does he react to frustrations or to unpleasant situations? 33. Is he emotionally calm or excitable? 35. Does he act impulsively or cautiously? In each case the subject was rated on a five-point scale.

not in agreement with the findings of Line and Griffin (94), who report a higher color score for their stable group than for their unstable group. This later study is not strictly comparable, since the writers made no attempt to study the balance between the various types of color responses or their relationship to the other determinants.

A third hypothesis underlying the total personality picture of an individual as revealed by the Rorschach Test is concerned with P responses. These are said to indicate the individual's ability to think as others do and to conform to the accepted social mores. If this hypothesis is valid, then the subjects in this study who received relatively low ratings on the Olson Behavior Rating Scale should give a higher number of P responses than subjects whose ratings were relatively high, since a high score on the Olson scale indicates the presence of nonconformist behavior tendencies. That this was not the case is shown by the correlation of $-.071$ ($k_r = 0.78$) between the score on the Olson scale and the number of P responses. It is to be recalled, however, that P responses in this study were scored on adolescent and adult norms, so that the lack of validity of P as here indicated means merely that P responses, given by young children and scored on the basis of adolescent-adult norms, are not related to social conformity as measured by the Olson scale. It is quite possible that if norms for P responses given by young children had been available, the results would have been different. This again emphasizes the need for norms for young children before many of the basic assumptions underlying the Rorschach Test can be checked adequately at this age level.

It is claimed that the Rorschach Test gives a picture of an individual's usual manner of solving problems. The *Erfassungstyp*, or manner of approach, depends upon the relationship between W, D, and Dr responses. It is generally agreed that the most common pattern in the adult is represented by 25 per cent to 30 per cent W responses, 65 per cent to 70 per cent D responses, and approximately 10 per cent Dr responses. This pattern is symbolized W-D-Dr. All manner of variation from the usual pattern may occur. For example, the individual may overstress W responses but still include some D and Dr responses in his record (*W*-D-Dr), or he may overstress Dr responses, at the same time giving some W and D responses (W-D-*Dr*). The percentages of children showing various kinds of *Erfassungstyp* are presented in Table 22. The possible variations of *Erfassungstyp* are numerous, and the number of cases in this investigation is too small to make other than a rough indication of the manner of approach possible. For example, the subject who stresses W may do so to a greater or less degree. In either case he may or may not do this to the exclusion of Dr responses. The degree to which a determinant is overstressed or understressed, as well as its relationship to the other determinants, is important in the interpretation of an individual record but cannot be analyzed in this study, where the consideration of group trends is primary.

Table 22 indicates that only a small proportion of the young children in this study approximates the usual adult pattern in

TABLE 22.—PERCENTAGE OF BOYS AND GIRLS SHOWING VARIOUS ERFASSUNGSTYPEN IN RELATION TO CHRONOLOGICAL AGE

Chronological age	*3-0 to 5-11*			*6-0 to 7-11*		
Sex	*Boys*	*Girls*	*Both*	*Boys*	*Girls*	*Both*
Subjects	*36*	*41*	*77*	*21*	*25*	*46*
ERFASSUNGSTYP						
W-D-Dr	8	10	9	19	16	17
$\underline{W}$-D-Dr or $\underline{W}$-D	42	49	45	19	20	20
$\overline{W}$-$\underline{D}$-Dr or $\overline{W}$-$\underline{D}$	14	15	14	14	20	17
W-$\overline{D}$-$\underline{Dr}$	22	15	18	43	36	39
$\underline{W}$-D-$\underline{Dr}$	11	12	12	5	4	4
$\overline{W}$-$\underline{D}$-$\underline{Dr}$	3	0	1	0	4	2

manner of approach. There was a tendency for slightly more of the older children than of the younger to follow this pattern (*CR* 1.25). The typical approach of the preschool children seemed to be a tendency to emphasize W responses to a greater or less degree. In all cases some D responses were given but 60 per cent of the preschool children and 44 per cent of the older children stressed W to the exclusion of Dr responses. Almost one half of the younger children, in contrast to one fifth of the older children, used this manner of approach (*CR* 3.05). In an adult this manner of approach is thought to indicate a person of above average intelligence who can think abstractly, theoretically, and philosophically, and yet is able to maintain his contact with reality (26). This interpretation has little meaning if applied to young children without some modification. As has been pointed out previously, W responses given by young children are often of poor quality, being either arbitrary or confabulatory responses.* The W responses which are of good quality are more apt to be structural than combinatory W's.†

The interpretation of *Erfassungstyp* in young children must wait for further refinement in the meanings of W, D, and Dr responses at this age level. At the present time about all that can be said is that approximately half the preschool children in the present study tended to attack problems as a whole and to give a quick solution more or less uninhibited by details which were inconsistent with the given solution. The manner of approach of the older children, on the other hand, was characterized by emphasis of rare details, but in no case was this emphasis so great as to exclude some W and D responses. W responses given by the older children were apt to be based on good form perception. The finding that preschool children approach problems as wholes and that slightly older children seem overconcerned with the many—and often rare—details again suggests that the Rorschach method, if applied to a large group of children of varying ages, might contribute greatly to our understanding of the development of logical thinking. If the above findings are verified, it would be interesting to study older children to determine how and when the ability to organize details into meaningful wholes develops. For example, does the older child pass through a period when wholes are again emphasized before he approaches the adult pattern, or is the approach to this pattern gradually made without this intermediate stage?

Related to the question of an individual's manner of approach is the question of the consistency with which the chosen method of attack is followed. In the Rorschach Test the sequence between W, D, and Dr responses is claimed to indicate the individual's consistency or lack of consistency in approaching a problem. Rorschach distinguished five types of sequence: rigid, orderly, inverse, loose, and confused.‡ The determination

* Arbitrary responses are interpretations assigned to the blot without consideration for its essential features. Confabulatory responses are DW responses.

† Structural W's require little organization since they are based primarily on the obvious form of the blot, whereas combinatory W's require considerable analysis and synthesis of the various parts into a meaningful whole.

‡ *Rigid* sequence: The subject follows closely the patterns W-D-Dr or D-Dr. *Orderly* sequence: The subject follows the above patterns in general but varies the sequence on occasion. *Inverse* sequence: The subject follows the pattern Dr-D-W. *Loose* sequence: The subject follows no one pattern consistently but some system is apparent. *Confused* sequence: The subject follows no pattern and no system is apparent.

of sequence is difficult and often impossible in the records of young children because their responses are often quite limited in number. As far as could be determined, no child in this study followed a rigid or an inverse sequence. A rigid sequence would be unlikely to occur in the records of superior young children, but because of the tendency of many of the 6- and 7-year-olds to emphasize rare details, some evidence of inverse sequences might reasonably have been expected. Many records were so close to the borderline between orderly and loose and between loose and confused that sequences could not be determined with accuracy. For this reason the writer is unwilling to commit herself to the extent of giving proportions of children in relation to sequence. It may be said, however, that the young children in this study tended to follow a loose rather than an orderly sequence except for a few cases in which the sequence could probably best be described as confused. The general tendency seemed to be for loose sequences to decrease and orderly sequences to increase with increasing chronological age.

This chapter does not attempt to cover all the many interrelationships on which the Rorschach personality picture is based. Such an attempt would be untimely since the testing of assumptions underlying these relationships cannot be undertaken until the determinants themselves are more clearly defined and understood. In this connection the findings of the present study make one further contribution. The Rorschach Test is said to give a measure of the constriction or flexibility of the total personality. While the measurement of constriction depends upon the interrelation of many variables, it is based primarily on %F. Rorschach workers are generally agreed that $\%F<50$ indicates flexibility; $\%F=50\text{–}80$ indicates varying degrees of constriction; and $\%F>80$ indicates extreme rigidity found only in pathological cases. If this hypothesis is valid in relation to young children, then a large majority of the records in the present study should show $\%F<50$. That such is not the case has already been indicated in Chapter VIII; the mean %F was greater than 70 at each age level. For the 3- and 4-year-olds the mean %F was greater than 80. Obviously the average child in this study is not constricted and certainly the average 3- or 4-year-old is not pathological. It was also shown that %F decreases with increasing chronological and mental age. Therefore modification of the hypothesis of constriction seems desirable in relation to the use of the test with young children. On the other hand, psychological constriction often involves a tendency to regress to the childhood pattern; hence the findings in the present study may actually be quite in accord with this theory. If this is the case, then the determination of the degree of constriction in early childhood becomes a measure of the child's level of maturity, and one would expect that a high degree of constriction would be present in the early years.

XIII. SUMMARY AND CONCLUSIONS

Summary

The Rorschach Inkblot Test was developed in 1921 by the Swiss psychiatrist Hermann Rorschach. The test consists of 10 bilaterally symmetrical inkblot designs centered on individual, stiff, white cards. In 5 of the blots only black ink is used; in 2 blots red and black ink are used; and in 3 blots several colored inks are used. The cards are numbered and are always presented in the same order. The technique of administering the test is essentially the same as that for any other individual test. Responses to the inkblots are scored in four principal categories: the manner of apperception, the quality of the response, the content of the response, and the degree of originality. The Rorschach Test is claimed to give a comprehensive picture of the total personality, revealing both intellectual and nonintellectual traits and the functional interaction between them. The test is unique in that the same material may be used from early childhood through the adult years.

In recent years the Rorschach Test has been used increasingly with preschool children, but up to the present time no attempt has been made to check the reliability of the test or to validate any of the test determinants at the preschool level. Nor has there been any detailed publication of the results of Rorschach records of preschool children. The purposes of the present study were to simplify and refine administrative procedures so that they would be meaningful to young children; to analyze variation in test determinants in terms of chronological age, mental age, and sex and to present these findings as a tentative basis for future standardization of the test in its application to young children; to study the reliability of the test determinants at the preschool level; and to check the validity of certain specific claims made by Rorschach as to the meanings of the various test determinants. It is essentially an exploratory study and as such should raise more questions than it attempts to answer.

The 123 subjects in this study ranged in age between 3 and 8 years and there were approximately as many boys as girls. At the time of their tests the 77 preschool children were enrolled in one of the following groups: the University of Minnesota nursery school or kindergarten, Northrop Collegiate nursery school or kindergarten, or the nursery school of the New York State College of Home Economics at Cornell University. The 46 older children were enrolled in the first or second grades of either Northrop Collegiate School in Minneapolis or Cayuga Heights School in Ithaca. Fifty-five of the preschool children were given retests approximately one month after the initial tests. Stanford-Binet (Form L) records were available for each of the 123 children. In addition to the mental test records, teachers' ratings of each child were secured on the Olson Behavior Rating Scale (Schedule B). Teachers' ratings for 30 of the preschool children were secured on the Marston Introversion-Extroversion Rating Scale. The subjects in this study constitute a highly homogeneous group both in intelligence and in socio-economic status.

In so far as possible the testing setup was arranged to secure the maximum cooperation of the child. All tests were given in the school building in a room free from distractions. Records were taken during the morning, shortly after the child's arrival at school, thus minimizing the fatigue and hunger factors. All children had had many contacts with the writer during the normal school day. In general, the administrative technique described by Rorschach was followed, but the age of the subjects made certain modifications necessary. The cards were presented in an upright position and the child was not permitted to rotate them. A second modification that seemed desirable was the introduction of a trial inkblot preceding the test. After considerable preliminary experimentation, simplified instructions were adopted.

In scoring the records in this study the writer followed Rorschach's original instructions, supplemented by the work of Beck, Hertz, and Rickers. The undesirability of scoring the records of young children on the basis of the adult norms was recognized but, since no norms for young children have yet been developed, there was no alternative.

Findings

1. The data in the present study support the claim made by Klopfer and Margulies that three successive stages of early Rorschach reactions may be defined in the records of young

children. In addition, the writer defined a further stage and suggested terms for designating the stages which Klopfer and Margulies defined but merely described as patterns A, B, and C. The four stages of early reactions were designated the pre-logic stage, the confused-logic stage, the perseverated-logic stage, and the true-logic stage.

2. The percentage of children rejecting at least one card in the Rorschach series decreased from 32 at 3 years, 18.5 at 4 years, and 8 at 5 years to 0 at 6 and 7 years.

3. One of the major difficulties involved in the use of the Rorschach Test with young children at the present time is the lack of norms on which to base interpretations. The present study, while not a normative one, makes a distinct contribution in this area in that the responses of a highly homogeneous group of young children are analyzed in terms of age. This analysis indicated that many of the determinants on which the total personality picture depends are closely related to the age of the subject. The following determinants were found to increase markedly with increasing chronological age: R, Obj, D, F, F+, %F+, %M+, %O+, and OL (a scoring category introduced here for the first time). The following determinants increased with increasing chronological age but the increase was less marked: Dr, %D, %Dr, M, %M, M+, P, O, O+, %P, and %O. While %W and %F decreased with increasing chronological age, W, C (including C, CF, and FC), %C (including %C, %CF, and %FC), %A, and reaction time showed almost no variation with chronological age.

4. In terms of percentage of children using the determinants, M and FM responses increased with increasing chronological age. At each age level the percentage of children giving FM responses was greater than the percentage of children giving M responses. The incidence of m responses was too infrequent and too irregular to warrant any interpretation at the age level of the young child.

5. There was a general tendency for the number of children using C, CF, and FC responses to increase with increasing chronological age. The percentage of children giving CF responses was higher than the percentage of children giving C and FC responses at each age level, except at 5 years, where the percentage giving FC responses was higher. The percentage giving Cn responses decreased markedly with increasing chronological

age. If Cn responses are included in C responses, as is the custom with many Rorschach workers, then C responses predominate between 3 and 5 years and CF responses predominate at 6 and 7 years. Within the age range of this study the behavior of the various color determinants is in line with the generally accepted hypothesis that C responses are indicative of uninhibited emotionality, CF responses indicative of a tendency for emotions to predominate, and FC responses indicative of emotional adjustment. According to this hypothesis, one would expect C responses to predominate during early childhood, CF responses to predominate somewhat later, and FC responses to predominate still later. This is what does happen except that within the age range of this study CF responses continue to predominate.

6. The content of the responses showed little relationship to age except that with increasing age a wider range of content appeared. The three major content categories were animal, nature, and human. The increase in human responses between 5 and 7 years could be attributed largely to an increase in responses interpreted as fairies, elves, and other imaginary characters.

7. In terms of mean number and mean percentage of occurrence, no sex differences were apparent in this study. The similarity between means for boys and girls was marked, and in all cases the variation within a sex group was greater than the slight variation between groups.

8. Certain sex differences were apparent, however, in terms of age at which the determinants were utilized. The preschool boys tended to give M and FM responses earlier than preschool girls, and preschool girls tended to give color responses earlier than preschool boys. In the older group these sex differences tended to disappear.

9. The test-retest reliabilities of the Rorschach Test determinants ranged from +.38 to +.86. Each relationship was above the 1 per cent level of significance. When reliabilities were calculated by the split-half method and corrected by the Spearman-Brown formula, the reliabilities of the various determinants ranged from +.02 to +.91. Except in the case of %W and %D, the split-half reliabilities of the initial test and the retest were quite comparable, and the uncorrected coefficients were above the 1 per cent level of significance.

10. The data in the present study do not support Rorschach's claim in respect to the relationship between W and intellectual level, as is indicated by the correlation of +.103 between W and mental age. They do support Rorschach's claim in respect to M, %F+, C-sum, and %O+, as shown by the correlations of +.581, +.612, +.252, and +.580 between mental age and M, %F+, C-sum, and %O+ respectively. The correlation of +.070 between %A and mental age does not support Rorschach's claim of an inverse relationship. In addition to the above determinants, R, Obj, and OL were even more closely related to mental age. This is indicated by the correlations of +.634, +.680, and +.684 between mental age and R, Obj, and OL respectively. The relationships between the above determinants and IQ were considerably lower than the relationships between these determinants and mental age. This discrepancy may be accounted for by the fact that the determinants were shown to increase with chronological age as well as with mental age. Since the chronological age of the very superior group was slightly lower than that of the superior group, this would have the effect of lowering the relationship between the various determinants and IQ.

11. As measured by the M:C-sum ratio, the percentage of young children showing introversive tendencies increased with increasing chronological age and the percentage showing extratensive tendencies decreased with increasing chronological age. More boys than girls showed introversive tendencies at 3 years, and this relationship continued until between 5 and 6 years, when it was reversed.

12. The correspondence between introversive-extratensive tendencies as measured by the M:C-sum ratio and the Marston Introversion-Extroversion Scale was 60 per cent. When the determination of *Erlebnistyp* was based on the M:C-sum ratio, supplemented and checked by the R(VIII–X):R ratio, the correspondence between this measure and the Marston scale was increased to 73 per cent.

13. The correspondence between *Erlebnistyp*, as measured by the M: C-sum ratio, on first and second tests was 71 per cent. The correlation between R(VIII–X):R, based on first and second tests, was +.375. When the latter ratio was used to supplement the former in the determination of *Erlebnistyp*, the agreement between first and second tests was 82 per cent.

14. Rorschach's claim that color responses give a measure of the individual's emotional adjustment is supported by the finding of $C=.50$ between teachers' ratings on four items of the Olson Behavior Rating Scale and emotional adjustment as indicated by color responses in the Rorschach Test.

15. Rorschach's claim that P responses are indicative of the individual's tendency to conform to group standards is not supported by the present data. This is shown by the correlation of $-.071$ between scores on the Olson scale and the number of P responses. The lack of validity of P means merely that P responses, given by young children and scored on the basis of adolescent-adult norms, were not related to social conformity as measured by the Olson scale.

16. Only a small proportion of the children in this study approximated the usual adult *Erfassungstyp*. There was a tendency for slightly more older children than younger to approximate this pattern. The typical approach of the preschool children was an emphasis on W responses to a greater or less degree. The manner of approach of the older children was an emphasis on Dr responses, but in no case was the emphasis so great as to exclude some W and D responses.

17. The determination of sequence was difficult and often impossible. As far as could be determined, no child in the present study followed a rigid or inverse sequence. In most cases the sequence was loose rather than orderly, with a few cases in which the sequence can best be described as confused. There was a tendency for loose sequences to decrease and orderly sequences to increase with increasing chronological age.

Conclusions

1. The Rorschach Test, when administered under the conditions outlined in this study, is applicable to young children 3 years and older. This is indicated not only by their interest and cooperation in responding to the cards but also by the marked variety of their responses. The use of the test with children younger than 3 years is possible, but many incomplete records are to be expected. Even when complete records are secured, the problems involved in scoring and interpretation are so great that the contribution of such records becomes questionable.

2. Young children utilize all the ways of responding to the

Rorschach inkblots which are utilized by adults, but not to the same extent.

3. Adequate norms for the Rorschach Test determinants are needed before the test can be used with maximum efficiency with young children. These norms need to be in terms of year or half-year intervals rather than for young children or even preschool children as a group.

4. The test-retest reliability coefficients, although not uniformly high for each determinant, are quite comparable to those reported by other investigators for older subjects. The findings of the present study suggest that with further refinement of procedure and scoring, the reliabilities of the various test determinants may be expected to approximate those of other standard tests for young children. Even at the present time, under the conditions set up in this study, the reliabilities of most of the determinants are fairly satisfactory, especially when one considers that these reliabilities are based on a highly homogeneous group and that the interpretation of test results does not depend upon any one determinant but upon the balance and interrelationship between determinants.

5. The validity of some of the interpretative principles underlying the use of the Rorschach Test is substantiated, in part, by the following data:

a. M, %F+, %O+, and C-sum are directly related to intelligence as measured by the Stanford-Binet test.

b. The measurement of introversive-extratensive tendencies by the M:C-sum ratio is in fair agreement with the measurement of introversion-extroversion by the Marston scale. Supplementing the M:C-sum ratio with the R(VIII–X):R ratio increases the percentage of agreement between introversion-extroversion as measured by these combined ratios and by the Marston scale.

c. The determination of emotional adjustment as measured by color responses is in fair agreement with emotional adjustment as indicated by teachers' ratings on four items of the Olson scale.

6. That certain modifications of interpretative principles are necessary when the Rorschach Test is applied to young children is indicated by the following data:

a. At the level of the young child W is not related to intelligence, whereas R, Obj, and OL (a determinant introduced here for the first time) are more closely related to intelligence, as measured by the Stanford-Binet test, than any of the other determinants except %F+.

b. P responses, given by young children and scored on the basis of adolescent-adult norms, are not related to social conformity as measured by the Olson scale. Whether or not P responses are related to social conformity when they are scored on the basis of norms for young children is, of course, still an open question.

c. Because of the very high %F found in the records of young children, some modification of Rorschach's theory of constriction is necessary when the test is used with young children.

Suggestions for Future Study

1. A study of the effect of the stationary position versus free rotation on the test results of young children.

2. A study of the effect of combining the initial presentation of the cards and the inquiry when the test is used with young children. In this study one of the major difficulties was the tendency for children to lose interest after the initial presentation of the series and, consequently, to object to the inquiry. If the inquiry could follow each card, without unduly influencing the succession, a real contribution to ease of administration would result.

3. The standardization of a simple trial blot is needed so that pretest conditions may be similar for all subjects.

4. Further study is needed to ascertain more accurately the lower age limits of test usefulness.

5. The outstanding need at the present time is a normative study at the level of the young child.

6. Since W responses given by young children differ in quality from those given by adults, a study of the structure of W responses given by children is very much needed.

7. A further and more extensive analysis of the development of the various color responses with an attempt to validate the hypotheses underlying the interpretation of C, CF, and FC responses would be desirable.

8. A further study of the development of movement responses with an attempt to validate the hypotheses underlying the interpretation of M, FM, and m responses is also needed.

9. It has been suggested earlier in this study that the Ror-

schach Test be used as a method for studying the development of logical thinking in young children.

10. Particularly needed at the present time is a series of sample Rorschach responses of young children. These examples should include Rorschach records of deviates as well as the records of average children of various ages.

11. A study of Rorschach records of young children in relation to extensive case histories of these children is essential for adequate validation.

12. A longitudinal study of successive Rorschach records of a group of normal children would provide some greatly needed evidence on the important question of prediction.

APPENDIX A

Items within the Content Classifications

1. *Animal.* Since approximately 40 per cent of the total responses fell within the animal classification (not including animal detail), a more detailed analysis is possible than in the other content classifications.

Items within the Animal Classification
(Analysis of Items According to Number of Children Using Them)

25 and above	*15–24*	*5–14*		*Under 5*	
butterfly	bug	fish	pig	lamb	ant
bird	spider	chicken	beetle	moth	toad
dog	lion	bat	elephant	grasshopper	turkey
bear	mouse	duck	turtle	fox	stork
rabbit	cat	fly	tiger	dragon	rhinoceros
monkey	frog	wolf	owl	donkey	skunk
animal (not specified)		deer	squirrel	giraffe	beaver
		crab	bee	seal	pelican
		cow	caterpillar	alligator	buffalo
		sheep	snake	eagle	eel
		horse	worm	goat	camel
				zebra	crocodile
				goose	

2. *Animal detail.* Included in this category were all animal parts. Leg, foot, arm, finger, and head items were interpreted as belonging to various specific animals or were designated merely as belonging to animals. Deer horns, cat whiskers, claws, tails, beaks, feelers, stingers, elephant trunks, and wings of birds and butterflies were other items in this classification.

3. *Human.* People, man, lady, and girls were the most frequently mentioned items in this classification. With increasing age the number of fairy and witch interpretations increased. Also associated with increasing age was a tendency for the number of generalized human concepts, such as man or people, to decrease. Accompanying this decrease was an increase in more descriptive human interpretations, such as baby, children, funny men, old men, old ladies, little men, firemen, clowns, and Indians. Other items in this category were boy, little girl, silly men, bad boy, naughty girl, wicked women, mother and daddy, dancing lady, dancing man, candlestick maker, Eskimo, butler, Santa Claus, gingerbread boy, brownie, elf, dwarf, goblin, troll, ghost, and angel.

4. *Human detail.* Human faces were mentioned most frequently in this category. Leg, foot, arm, hand, and finger were also frequent responses. Less frequent were nose, eye, mouth, ear, and hair.

5. *Nature.* Since the most frequently mentioned items within this and the following classifications are mentioned in Chapter VIII, items will be enumerated in order of approximate frequency. Trees, flowers, leaves, fire, clouds, sun, snow, smoke, branches, raindrops, plants, bushes, grass, icicle, sunsets, nests, tree stumps, sunshine, weeds, rainbows, moon, stars, cocoons, roots, toadstools, thorns, and beehives.

6. *Objects.* Included in this classification were beds, chairs, candles, trains, boats, sticks, airplanes, flowerpots, guns, saws, cars, masks, lamps, bells, ball of string, hinges, teapots, vases, scarecrows, knockers, umbrellas, clothespins, pipes, train tracks, baskets, tables, hatchets, sprinklers, rockets, parachutes, matches, bathtubs, barrels, sleighs, totem poles, and rugs.

7. *Food and clothing.* Included in this classifieation were ice cream, hair ribbons, ice-cream cones, shoes, coats, dresses, candy suckers, hats, collars, slippers, socks, zippers, cookies, candy, scarves, gloves, carrots, milk, nuts, aprons, earmuffs, jelly, steak, and tuxedo.

8. *Toys.* Included in this classification were jack-o'-lantern, balls, snowmen, paper-dolls, teddy bears, dolls, puzzles, tricycles, swings, games, tops, balloons, boxing gloves, and merry-go-rounds.

9. *Architecture.* Included in this classification were houses, castles, bridges, tents, buildings, chimneys, churches, gates, water towers, porches, factories, smokestacks, steps, and doors.

10. *Landscape and seascape.* Included in this classification were mountains, rocks, water, oceans, villages, mud puddles, pools, hills, beaches, rivers, waterfalls, streams, lakes, islands, maps, and cemeteries. Also included were attempts to describe land or sea vistas, for example, "Here is a long, long road going over the hills and through the trees."

11. *Anatomy.* Included in this classification were blood, insides of stomachs, skeletons, wishbone, brains, muscles, ribs, bones inside, heart, breathing tubes, tubes to swallow, and broken teeth.

12. *Art.* Included in this classification were paints, statues, designs, decorations, Easter egg dye, Christmas trees, paintings, Valentine lace, violins, and song notes.

APPENDIX B

Sample Record of a Three-Year-Old

Case No. 5 (girl) . . . . . . CA 3-3 . . . . . . IQ 122

R.T.	*(sec.)*	*Response*	*Inquiry*	*Scoring*
I.	5	A dolly. (Points to D16.)	See, here is dolly. (Points to D16 again.)	D F+ Toy
II.	4	Some shoes. (Points to D14.)	(Frowns.) I told you shoes.	D F+Cl
III.	3	A monkey.	Here is the monkey. (D6)	D F+ A
		Ribbon. (Points to own ribbon.)	Just ribbon. (D7)	D F+Cl
IV.	3	A elephant didn't have no feet.	Funny elephant. (Rubs hand over whole blot.)	(1 OL) W F— A O—
V.	10	A cow.	A cow and that is all.	W F— A
VI.		What could it be? You tell me.	I told you no.	Refusal
VII.	6	A doggy. (Points to D3 and D5.)	Doggy has two tails, see. (Points to D1 and Dr4.)	D F— A
VIII.	3	Oh! Flowers—green, blue, pink, all kinds of colored flowers. (Smiles and pats card.)	These are the flowers. Pretty.	(1 OL) W CF+ Na
IX.	5	Green, orange, and pink. This could be a little house (points to Dr13) with flowers around it.	The flowers are all pink. (D9)	(Cn) (3 OL) D CF— Landsc
X.	3	A building. (Points to D6.)	I told you and that is all.	D F— Arch
		Here are two bells, see. (Points to D1 and 3.)		D F+ Obj

Sample Record of a Five-Year-Old

Case No. 59 (boy) ......CA 5-5......IQ 122

R. T. (sec.)	Response	Inquiry	Scoring
I. 5	Butterfly.	Just one butterfly.	W F+ A P
II. 4	Dog (points to D24), but where is the face?	The face is still gone.	(1 OL) D F+ A P
	A butterfly.	Here. (Points to D17.)	D F+ A
III. 25	Two fairies dancing.	Here they are. (Points to D6.)	(2 OL) D M+ H
	Some spilled blood.	Like when you prick your finger. (D3)	(1 OL) D CF+ Anat
IV. 4	Bat, but bats have bigger wings.	Just a bat.	(2 OL) W F+ A P
V. 3	It looks to me like a moth.	Just a moth.	W F+ A P
VI. 30	Alligator with a long neck.	Here. (W)	(2 OL) W F— A
VII. 17	Looks like mountains.	Just mountains.	W F— Landsc
	That could be water.	(DS11)	DS F+ Seasc
	Some ears.	Two ears. (D1)	D F+ Ad
VIII. 7	Bears climbing up mountains.	(W)	(FM) (2 OL) W M+ A P
	Two blue flags.	Here. (Points to D4.)	(1 OL) D FC+ Obj O+
IX. 6	Mountains (D11) and some trees (D8), with a road going up.	A road where you can drive.	(3 OL) W FC+ Landsc
X. 8	Castle.	(Points to D6.)	D F+ Arch O+
	Butterflies.	Here. (D10)	D F— A
	The crab (D4) is eating a fish (Dr2).		(FM) (2 OL) D M+ A

Sample Record of a Seven-Year-Old

Case No. 114 (boy) ......CA 7-2......IQ 133

R. T. (sec.)	Response	Inquiry	Scoring
I. 3	Looks like a spear. (D11)	Like an Indian spearhead.	D F+ Obj
	Well now, it looks like a seal. (D1)	Just the head.	Do F+ Ad
	Oh, it could be a jack-o'-lantern.		(1 OL) W(DS) F+ Toy
	A cliff with broken trees.	Top center (D2) projections.	(2 OL) Dr F— Na
II. 3	The red here looks like blood or fire. (D17)	It's red like blood or fire.	Na D C Anat
	Maybe a burning house or a burning monoplane. (W)	Can't tell about the house or plane but there is fire.	(1 OL) Obj W CF+ Arch
	Bugs. (D14)	Here. (D14)	D F— A
	This looks like clouds.	Gray clouds. (D24)	D KF+ Na

R. T. (sec.)		*Response*	*Inquiry*	*Scoring*
III.	3	A necktie. (D7)	To snap on.	D F+ Cl
		Old weeds or plants.	(D3)	(1 OL) D F− Na
		Looks like a crab.	(D5)	D F− A
		These look like pelicans.	I saw some in the zoo. (D6)	D F+ A
		Icicles.	(Dr11)	Dr F+ Na O+
IV.	2	A bug all together.	(W)	W F+ A
		See, this looks like the fins of a fish.	(Dr10)	Dr F− Ad
		These might be eyes of some kind of animal.	Top center (D2) projections.	Dr F+ Ad
V.	2	Looks like a butterfly.	(W)	W F+ A P
		These are like clouds.	(D2)	D KF− Na
		These are like plants pushing up the earth.	They are coming out. (D1)	(2 OL) D Fm+ Na
VI.	3	This is like a mass of clouds.	Storm clouds maybe. (D18)	D KF+ Na
		This looks like a magic Indian prayer stick. (D4)	I have one.	(3 OL) D F+ Art O+
		There really isn't much here.		
VII.	7	Looks like balanced snake.	(W)	(1 OL) W FK+ Na
		A clown's face.	Profile. (D3)	(1 OL) D F+ Hd P
VIII.	3	Looks like the Grand Canyon with all colored rocks. You see, I have traveled.	(W)	(2 OL) W FC+ Landsc O+
		You could say that here are diamonds (Dr6) and gold (D7) with a blue roof covering them—treasures.	D10 omitted from interpretation.	(5 OL) Obj D CF+ Arch O+
		Gosh, those bears are (D10) climbing.		(FM) (1 OL) D M+ A P
IX.	4	Here are rubies. (D27)		D C Obj
		This could be grass.	A green lawn.	D CF+ Na
X.	3	Just lots of bugs all crawling around.	(W)	(FM) (2 OL) W M− A
		Blue water (D4) splashing against a house (D6).		(3 OL) D FC+ m Landsc
		Eels. (D14)		D F− A
		These are cherries. (D5)		D F+ Na
		This is a partly burned tree trunk. (D19)	Just a stump left.	(2 OL) D F+ Na
		Leaves. (Dr13)		Dr F+ Na

GLOSSARY

Definitions of Rorschach Terminology as Used in This Study

Arbitrary response. An interpretation assigned to the card without consideration for its essential features.

Chiaroscuro response. A response determined at least in part by the various shading values of the card.

Color naming. A response in which colors are enumerated with no attempt at interpretation.

Color response. A response in which color is the primary or secondary determinant of the response.

Combinatory whole response. A whole response resulting from an analysis of the various parts of the card and the organization of these parts into a meaningful whole.

Confabulatory whole response. A response in which a single detail is used as the basis for the interpretation of the card as a whole.

Confused sequence. No pattern is followed by the subject in the sequence of W-D-Dr.

Constriction. Rigidity in psychological functioning.

Content of the response. The subject matter of the response, i.e., animal, human, nature, etc.

Detail response. A response based on frequently selected details of the card. Hertz designated as detail responses all responses to details which, in her group, were above the twentieth percentile in frequency.

Determinant. Specifically refers to how a concept is formed and therefore is descriptive of the quality of the response. In its wider meaning it is a general term descriptive of any of the Rorschach symbols.

Erfassungstyp. Manner of approach. Refers to the proportion of responses in each location category.

Erlebnistyp. Experience balance or experience type. Refers to the balance between introversive and extratensive tendencies.

Form response. A response in which the shape of the blot is the primary or secondary determinant of the response.

Inquiry. The subject is given a second opportunity to go through the Rorschach series and to elaborate his first responses. The major function of the inquiry is to assist the examiner in scoring and interpreting the record.

Inverse sequence. The subject tends to follow the sequence pattern Dr-D-W.

Location category. Same as manner of apperception. Refers to the area of the card which stimulates a particular response, i.e., W, D, Dr, etc.

Loose sequence. No one sequence pattern for W, D, and Dr responses is followed, but some system is apparent.

"Magic repetition." The same response is repeated for successive cards. This response may be determined by some rather vague impression received from the first card, or it may have no relation to even the first card.

Manner of apperception. Also called "mode of apperception." Refers to the location of the response, i.e., whether the stimulus is the whole card or some detail.

Movement response. A response which indicates an experience of felt movement.

Objects. The total number of persons or items mentioned in response to the Rorschach series. As far as can be determined, this is identical with Hertz's "items."

Oligophrenic detail response. A response to only a part of a human or animal when most people see the whole body clearly.

Orderly sequence. The usual pattern, W-D-Dr, is followed in general but is occasionally varied.

Organizational links. The number of verbalized, logical connections within a response or within a record.

Original response. A response given no more often than once in 100 tests.

Originality of the response. Refers to the uniqueness or popularity of the response.

Popular response. A response which is given once in six times to the whole card or to some detail within the card.

Quality of the response. Refers to the basis underlying the interpretation, i.e., form, movement, color, or shading or a combination of these.

Range of content. Number of subject matter classifications represented in an individual record.

Rare-detail response. A response based on rarely selected details of the card. Hertz designated all responses to details which, in her group, were below the twentieth percentile in frequency as rare-detail responses.

Reaction time. The time which elapses between the first presentation of the card and the first response.

Rigid sequence. The sequence pattern W-D-Dr or D-Dr is followed with marked consistency.

Space response. A response stimulated by the white spaces within or adjacent to the blots.

Structural whole response. A response which is based primarily on the obvious form of the total blot.

Trial blot. A homemade inkblot used to orient the subject before the presentation of the Rorschach series.

Whole response. A response to the card as a whole.

Rorschach Symbols and Their Meaning

A—animal. The card or some part of it is interpreted as a whole animal.

%A—per cent animal. $\frac{A+Ad}{R}$ multiplied by 100.

Ad—animal detail. The card or some part of it is interpreted as some part of an animal.

Anat—anatomy. The card or some part of it is interpreted in anatomical terms.

Arch—architecture. The card or some part of it is interpreted in architectural terms.

C—color. Color is the sole determinant of the response.

%C—per cent color. $\frac{C+CF+FC}{R}$ multiplied by 100.

CF—color form. Color constitutes the primary and form the secondary determinant of the response.

Cl—clothing. The card or some part of it is interpreted as an article of clothing.

Cn—color naming. Color is enumerated with no attempt at interpretation.

C-sum—color-sum. The number of C responses multiplied by 1.5 plus the number of CF responses multiplied by 1.0 plus the number of FC responses multiplied by 0.5.

D—detail. A response to frequently selected details of the card.

%D—per cent detail. $\frac{D}{R}$ multiplied by 100.

Do—oligophrenic detail. Only a part of a human or animal is interpreted when most subjects see the whole body clearly.

%Do—per cent oligophrenic detail. $\frac{Do}{R}$ multiplied by 100.

Dr—rare detail. A response to rarely selected details of the card.

%Dr—per cent detail. $\frac{Dr}{R}$ multiplied by 100.

DS—space detail. A response to white spaces within or adjacent to the blot.

%DS—per cent space detail. $\frac{DS}{R}$ multiplied by 100.

DW—detail-whole. The card is interpreted as a whole but the primary basis of the interpretation is some detail within the card.

%DW—per cent detail-whole. $\frac{DW}{R}$ multiplied by 100.

F—form. The shape of the blot is the sole determinant of the response.

%F—per cent form. $\frac{F}{R}$ multiplied by 100.

F+—good form. The interpretation is based on forms which are frequently seen and is consistent with the shape of the blot.

%F+—per cent good form. $\frac{F+}{F}$ multiplied by 100.

FC—form color. Form is the primary and color the secondary determinant of the response.

FM—animal motion. A feeling of movement is the determinant of the response which is interpreted as an animal in action.

Fo—food. The card or some part of it is interpreted as some kind of food.

H—human. The card or some part of it is interpreted as a human figure.

%H—per cent human. $\frac{H+Hd}{R}$ multiplied by 100.

Hd—human detail. The card or some part of it is interpreted as some part of a human figure.

K—chiaroscuro. The various shading values of the card determine the response.

M—movement. A feeling of movement is the determinant of the response which is interpreted as a human in action. Rorschach made no distinction between **M** and FM responses.

%M—per cent movement. $\frac{M}{R}$ multiplied by 100.

M+—good movement. Since movement always implies form in action, M+ indicates that the movement interpretation is based on forms which are frequently seen and is consistent with the shape of the blot.

%M+—per cent good movement. $\frac{M+}{M}$ multiplied by 100.

m—inanimate objects in motion.

Na—nature. The card or some part of it is interpreted in terms of nature.

O—original. A response which occurs no oftener than once in 100 tests.

%O—per cent original. $\frac{O}{R}$ multiplied by 100.

O+—good original. An original response based on good form perception.

%O+—per cent good original. $\frac{O+}{O}$ multiplied by 100.

Obj—object. The total number of persons or objects mentioned in responses to the Rorschach series. When Obj occurs in the content category, it means that the card or some part of it is interpreted as an object.

OL—organizational links. The number of verbalized, logical connections within a record.

P—popular. A response to the card or a part of the card which occurs at least once in every six records.

%P—per cent popular. $\frac{P}{R}$ multiplied by 100.

R—responses. The total number of responses to the Rorschach series.

R.T.—reaction time. The time between the first presentation of the card and the first response.

W—whole. A response to the card as a whole.

%W—per cent whole. $\frac{W}{R}$ multiplied by 100.

WS—whole-space. A response to the card as a whole, including the white spaces within and adjacent to the blot.

%WS—per cent whole-space. $\frac{WS}{R}$ multiplied by 100.

A Brief Summary of Some Conventional Interpretative Measures

The description of intellectual level depends on:

The number and quality of W
The number and quality of M
The proportion of good form perception (%F+)
The number and quality of O
The proportion of W, D, and Dr
Sequence of W, D, and Dr

The description of *Erlebnistyp* (experience balance between introversive-extratensive tendencies) depends on:
M : C-sum
(FM+m) : (Fc+c+C')
R (VIII–X) : R

The description of emotional development depends on:
The number of and relationship between C, CF, and FC responses
The number of and relationship between M and FM responses

Tendencies toward anxiety and insecurity are indicated by:
Number and quality of W
K in relation to the other determinants
Attitude of the individual in giving responses
Content of the responses

The description of the individual's ability to conform to social groups depends upon the number of P in relation to the other determinants.

The description of the degree and kind of control which an individual is able to exert over his spontaneous impulses depends on:
FC : (CF+C)
(FC+CF+C) : (Fc+c+C')
The number of M
The proportion of F (%F)
The relationship between C-sum, M, and %F

BIBLIOGRAPHY

1. Abramson, J. De deux tests d'imagination et d'observation. Journal de Psychologique, 24:370–79 (1927).
2. Andrews, Elizabeth. The development of imagination in the pre-school child. University of Iowa Studies in Character, Vol. III, No. 4. University of Iowa, 1930.
3. Bartlett, F. C. An experimental study of some problems of perceiving and imaging. British Journal of Psychology, 8:222–66 (1916).
4. Beck, S. J. Personality diagnosis by means of the Rorschach Test. American Journal of Orthopsychiatry, 1:81–88 (1930).
5. ———. The Rorschach Test and personality diagnosis. 1. Feebleminded. American Journal of Psychiatry, 10:19–52 (1930).
6. ———. The Rorschach Test in problem children. American Journal of Orthopsychiatry, 1:501–9 (1931).
7. ———. The Rorschach Test as applied to a feebleminded group. Archives of Psychology, Vol. XXI, No. 136 (1932).
8. ———. Configurational tendencies in Rorschach responses. American Journal of Psychology, 45:433–43 (1933).
9. ———. The Rorschach method and personality organization. 1. Balance and personality. American Journal of Psychiatry, 13:519–32 (1933).
10. ———. The Rorschach method and the organization of personality. II. Basic processes. American Journal of Orthopsychiatry, 3:361–75 (1933).
11. ———. The Rorschach method and personality organization. III. Psychological and social personality. American Journal of Orthopsychiatry, 4:290–97 (1934).
12. ———. Problems of further research in the Rorschach Test. American Journal of Orthopsychiatry, 5:100–15 (1935).
13. ———. Introduction to the Rorschach method: a manual of personality study. American Orthopsychiatric Association, Monograph 1 (1937).
14. ———. Psychological processes in Rorschach findings. Journal of Abnormal and Social Psychology, 31:482–88 (1937).
15. ———. Some recent Rorschach problems. Rorschach Research Exchange, 2 :15–22 (1937–38).
16. ———. Sources of error in Rorschach Test procedure. Psychological Bulletin, 37:516–17 (1940).
17. Behn-Eschenburg, H. Psychische Schüleruntersuchungen mit dem Formdeutversuch. Ernst Bircher, Bern, 1921.
18. Benjamin, J., and F. G. Ebaugh. The diagnostic validity of the Rorschach Test. American Journal of Psychiatry, 94:1163–78 (1938).
19. Binder, H. Die Helldunkeldeutungen im psychodiagnostischen Experiment von Rorschach. Orell Fussli, Zurich, 1932.
20. ———. The "light-dark" interpretations in Rorschach's experiment. Rorschach Research Exchange, 2:37–42 (1937–38).
21. Binet, A., and V. Henri. La psychologie individuelle. L'Année Psychologique, 2:411–65 (1895–96).
22. Birzele, K. Das Reproduzieren von Bildgestalten als Hilfsmittel zur Charakterbestimmung. Industrielle Psychotechnik, 15:65–78 (1938). Psychological Abstracts, 12:6466 (1938).
23. Bleuler, M. Der Rorschachsche Formdeuteversuch bei Geschwistern. Zeitschrift für die gesamte Neurologie und Psychiatrie, 118:366–98 (1929).
24. ———. Der Rorschach-Versuch als Unterscheidungsmittel von Konstitution und Prozess. Zeitschrift für die gesamte Neurologie und Psychiatrie, 151:571–78 (1934).
25. Bleuler, M., and R. Bleuler. Rorschach's Ink-Blot Test and racial psychology. Character and Personality, 4:97–114 (1935).
26. Bochner, Ruth, and Florence Halpern. The clinical application of the Rorschach Test. Grune and Stratton, New York, 1942.

27. Booth, G. C. Objective techniques in personality testing. Archives of Neural Psychiatry, 42:514–30 (1939).
28. Brian, Clara R., and Florence Goodenough. Relative potency of color and form perception at various ages. Journal of Experimental Psychology, 12:197–213 (1929).
29. Brosin, H. W., and Erika O. Fromm. Rorschach and color blindness. Rorschach Research Exchange, 4:39–70 (1940).
30. Burks, Barbara, and Mary C. Jones. Personality development in childhood: a survey of problems, methods, and experimental findings (Society Research in Child Development, Monograph 1). 1936.
31. Davidson, Helen H., and B. Klopfer. Rorschach statistics. Part I, Mentally retarded, normal and superior adults. Rorschach Research Exchange, 2:164–69 (1937–38).
32. ————. Rorschach statistics. Part II, Normal Children. Rorschach Research Exchange, 3:37–43 (1938–39).
33. Dearborn, G. V. Blots of ink in experimental psychology. Psychological Review, 4:390–91 (1897).
34. ————. A study of imagination. American Journal of Psychology, 9:183–90 (1898).
35. Dubitscher, F. Der Rorschachsche Formdeuteversuch als diagnostisches Hilfsmittel. Zeitschrift für die gesamte Neurologie und Psychiatrie, 138:515–35 (1932).
36. ————. Der Rorschachsche Formendeuteversuch bei erwachsenen Psychopathischen und schwachsinnigen Kindern. Zeitschrift für die gesamte Neurologie und Psychiatrie, 142:129–58 (1932).
37. ————. Die Persönlichkeitsentwicklung des Schulkindes in Rorschachischen Formdeuteversuch. Zeitschrift für Kinderforsch, 41:485–95 (1933).
38. Dunmire, Harriett. An evaluation of Beck's norms as applied to young children. (Paper read before Midwestern Psychological Association, 1939.) Psychological Bulletin, 36:629 (1939).
39. Dworetzki, G. Le test de Rorschach et l'évolution de la perception. Archives de Psychologie, 27:233–96 (1939).
40. Earl, C. J. A note on the validity of certain Rorschach symbols. Rorschach Research Exchange, 5:51–61 (1941).
41. Enke, W. Die Konstitutiontypen im Rorschachschen Experiment. Zeitschrift für die gesamte Neurologie und Psychiatrie, 108:645–74 (1927).
42. Fosberg, I. A. Rorschach reactions under varied instructions. Rorschach Research Exchange, 3:12–30 (1938–39).
43. ————. An experimental study of the reliability of the Rorschach technique. Rorschach Research Exchange, 5:72–84 (1941).
44. Frank, L. K. Comments on the proposed standardization of the Rorschach method. Rorschach Research Exchange, 3:101–5 (1938–39).
45. ————. Projective methods for the study of personality. Journal of Psychology, 8:389–413 (1939).
46. Gair, Mollie. Rorschach characteristics of a group of very superior seven year old children. Rorschach Research Exchange, 8:31–37 (1944).
47. Ganz, E. and M. Loosli-Usteri. Le test de Rorschach appliqué à 43 garçons anormaux. Archives de Psychologie, 24:245–55 (1934).
48. Gardner, G. E. Rorschach Test replies and results in 100 normal adults of average I.Q. American Journal of Orthopsychiatry, 6:32–60 (1936).
49. Guilford, J. P. Introversion-extroversion. Psychological Bulletin, 31:331–54 (1934).
50. Guirdham, A. On the value of the Rorschach Test. Journal of Mental Science, 81:848–69 (1935).
51. ————. The diagnosis of depression by the Rorschach Test. British Journal of Medical Psychology, 16:130–45 (1936).
52. Hallowell, A. I. The Rorschach Test as a tool for investigating cultural variables and individual differences in the study of personality in primitive societies. Rorschach Research Exchange, 5:31–34 (1941).
53. Harriman, P. L. The Rorschach Test applied to a group of college students. American Journal of Orthopsychiatry, 5:116–20 (1935).

54. HARROWER-ERICKSON, MARY R. The contributions of the Rorschach method to war-time psychological problems. Journal of Mental Science, 86:366–77 (1940).
55. ———. Direction for administration of the Rorschach Group Test. Rorschach Research Exchange, 5:145–53 (1941).
56. ———. Modification of the Rorschach method for use as a group test. Rorschach Research Exchange, 5:130–44 (1941).
57. HERTZ, MARGUERITE H. The Rorschach Ink-Blot Test. Unpublished dissertation, Western Reserve University, 1933.
58. ———. The reliability of the Rorschach Ink-Blot Test. Journal of Applied Psychology, 18:461–77 (1934).
59. ———. The Rorschach Ink-Blot Test: historical summary. Psychological Bulletin, 32:33–66 (1935).
60. ———. Rorschach norms for an adolescent group. Child Development, 6:69–76 (1935).
61. ———. Frequency tables to be used in scoring the Rorschach Ink-Blot Test. (Brush Foundation.) Western Reserve University, 1936.
62. ———. The method of administration of the Rorschach Ink-Blot Test. Child Development, 7:237–54 (1936).
63. ———. The "popular" response factor in the Rorschach scoring. Journal of Psychology, 6:3–31 (1938)
64. ———. Scoring the Rorschach Ink-Blot Test. Journal of Genetic Psychology, 52:15–64 (1938).
65. ———. Scoring the Rorschach Test with specific reference to "normal detail" category. American Journal of Orthopsychiatry, 8:100–21 (1938).
66. ———. On the standardization of the Rorschach method. Rorschach Research Exchange, 3:120–33 (1938–39).
67. ———. Percentage charts for use in computing Rorschach scores. (Brush Foundation and the Department of Psychology) Western Reserve University, 1940.
68. ———. Rorschach: twenty years after. Rorschach Research Exchange, 5:90–129 (1941).
69. HERTZ, MARGUERITE H., and ELIZABETH H. EBERT. The mental procedure of 6 and 8 year old children as revealed by the Rorschach inkblot method. Rorschach Research Exchange, 8:10–30 (1944).
70. HERTZ, MARGUERITE H., and B. RUBENSTEIN. A comparison of three "blind" Rorschach analyses. American Journal of Orthopsychiatry, 9:295–315 (1939).
71. HOROWITZ, R., and LOIS B. MURPHY. Projective methods in the psychological study of children. Journal of Experimental Education, 7:133–40 (1938).
72. HUNTER, M. Responses of comparable white and negro adults to the Rorschach Test. Journal of Psychology, 3:173–82 (1937).
73. ———. The practical value of the Rorschach Test in a psychological clinic. American Journal of Orthopsychiatry, 9:287–95 (1939).
74. KAPLAN, A. H., FLORENCE R. MIALE, and HAZEL CLAPP. Clinical validation of a Rorschach interpretation. Rorschach Research Exchange, 2:153–63 (1937–38).
75. KAY, LILLIAN W., and PAULINE G. VORHAUS. Rorschach reactions in early childhood. Part II, Intellectual aspects of personality development. Rorschach Research Exchange, 7:71–77 (1943).
76. KELLY, D. M., and S. E. BARRERA. The present state of the Rorschach method as a psychiatric adjunct. Rorschach Research Exchange, 4:30–36 (1940).
77. KERR, M. The Rorschach Test applied to children. British Journal of Psychology, 25:170–85 (1934).
78. KIRKPATRICK, E. Individual tests of school children. Psychological Research, 7:274–80 (1900).
79. KLOPFER, B. The present status of the theoretical development of the Rorschach method. Rorschach Research Exchange, 1:142–47 (1936–37).
80. ———. The technique of the Rorschach performance. Rorschach Research Exchange, 2:1–14 (1937–38).
81. ———. Should the Rorschach method be standardized? Rorschach Research Exchange, 3:45–54 (1938–39).
82. ———. Theory and technique of Rorschach interpretations. Rorschach Research Exchange, 3:152–94 (1938–39).

83. ———. Personality diagnosis in early childhood; application of the Rorschach method at the preschool level. Psychological Bulletin, 36:662 (1939).
84. ———. Personality differences between boys and girls in early childhood. Psychological Bulletin, 36:538 (1939).
85. Klopfer, B., and Helen Davidson. Record blanks for the Rorschach method of personality diagnosis. Rorschach Institute, Inc., New York, 1941.
86. Klopfer, B., Helen Davidson, *et al.* The technique of the Rorschach scoring and tabulation. Rorschach Research Exchange, 4:75–83 (1940).
87. Klopfer, B., and D. Kelley. The Rorschach technique: a manual for a projective method of personality diagnosis. World Book Co., New York, 1942.
88. Klopfer, B., and Helen Margulies. Rorschach reactions in early childhood. Rorschach Research Exchange, 5:1–23 (1941).
89. Klopfer, B., and Sadie Sender. A system of refined scoring symbols. Rorschach Research Exchange, 1:19–22 (1936–37).
90. Krugman, M. The Rorschach method. Character and Personality, 9:91–110 (1940).
91. Levy, D., and S. J. Beck. The Rorschach Test in manic-depressive psychosis. American Journal of Orthopsychiatry, 4:31–42 (1934).
92. Lewin, K. A dynamic theory of personality. McGraw-Hill, New York, 1935.
93. ———. Principles of topological psychology. McGraw-Hill, New York, 1936.
94. Line, W., and J. D. M. Griffin. Some results obtained with the Rorschach Test objectively scored. American Journal of Psychiatry, 92:109–14 (1935).
95. Loosli-Usteri, M. Le test de Rorschach appliqué à différents groupes d'enfants de 10–13 ans. Archives de Psychologie, 22:51–106 (1929).
96. ———. Le diagnostic individuel chez l'enfant au moyen du Test de Rorschach. Herman, Paris, 1937.
97. Lopfe, A. Über Rorschachische formdeuteversuche mit 10–13 jährigen Knaben. Zeitschrift für angewandte Psychologie, 26:202–53 (1925).
98. MacCalman, D. R. The Rorschach Test and its clinical application. Journal of Mental Science, 79:419–23 (1933).
99. Marston, L. R. The emotions of young children. University of Iowa Studies in Child Welfare, Vol. III, No. 3. University of Iowa, 1925.
100. Maza, A. L. Diagnóstico de niños anormales y superdotados. Revista de Pediologia, 10:412–17, 456–64 (1931).
101. Meltzer, H. Personality differences among stuttering children as indicated by the Rorschach Test. American Journal of Orthopsychiatry, 4:262–82 (1934).
102. ———. Talkativeness in stuttering and non-stuttering children. Journal of Genetic Psychology, 46:371–90 (1935).
103. Mira, L. E. Sobre et valor del Psicodiagnostico de Rorschach. Progressos de la Clinica, 30:808–45 (1925).
104. Monnier, M. Le test psychologique de Rorschach. Encéphale, 29:189–201, 247–70 (1934).
105. ———. La technique actuelle du test psychodiagnostique de Rorschach. Revision et criticism. Annales Médico-Psychologiques, 96:15–22 (1938).
106. Munroe, Ruth. The use of the Rorschach in college guidance. Rorschach Research Exchange, 4:107–30 (1940).
107. Murphy, Lois B. Personality development of a boy from age two to seven. American Journal of Orthopsychiatry, 14:10–21 (1944).
108. Oberholzer, E. Zur Differentialdiagnose psychischer Folgezustände nach Schädeltraumen mittels des Rorschachschen Formdeuteversuchs. Zeitschrift für die gesamte Neurologie und Psychiatrie, 136:596–620 (1931).
109. Oeser, O. A. Some experiments on the abstraction of form and color. II. Rorschach Tests. British Journal of Psychology, 22:287–323 (1932).
110. Olson, W. C. Problem tendencies in children. University of Minnesota Press, Minneapolis, 1930.
111. Parsons, C. J. Children's interpretations of ink-blots. British Journal of Psychology, 9:74–92 (1917).
112. Paulsen, Alma. Rorschachs of school beginners. Rorschach Research Exchange, 5:24–29 (1941).
113. Piotrowski, Z. On the Rorschach method and its application in organic disturbances of the central nervous system. Rorschach Research Exchange, 1:23–39 (1936–37).

114. ———. The M, FM, and m responses as indicators of changes in personality. Rorschach Research Exchange, 1:148–56 (1936–37).
115. ———. The methodological aspect of the Rorschach personality method. Kwartalnik Psychologiczny, 9:29–41 (1937).
116. ———. The reliability of Rorschach's Erlebnistypus. Journal of Abnormal and Social Psychology, 32:439–45 (1937).
117. ———. Recent Rorschach literature. Rorschach Research Exchange, 2:172–75 (1937–38).
118. Pyle, W. H. Examination of school children. Macmillan, New York, 1913.
119. Rickers-Ovsiankina, Maria. Rorschach scoring samples. Worcester State Hospital, Worcester, 1938.
120. ———. The Rorschach Test as applied to normal and schizophrenic subjects. British Journal of Medical Psychology, 17:227–57 (1938).
121. Rorschach, H. Psychodiagnostik (3d edition). Huber, Bern, 1937. A translation of this book was published in 1942 and is distributed by Grune and Stratton, New York. Page references in the text refer to the English translation.
122. Rorschach, H., and Z. Oberholzer. The application of the interpretation of form to psychoanalysis. Journal of Mental and Nervous Diseases, 60:225–48 (1924).
123. Rosenzweig, S. Outline of a cooperative project for validating the Rorschach Test. American Journal of Orthopsychiatry, 5:121–23 (1935).
124. Schachtel, Anna H. The Rorschach Test with young children. American Journal of Orthopsychiatry, 14:1–10 (1944).
125. Schneider, E. Die Bedeutung des Rorschachschen Formdeuteversuches zur Ermittlung intellektuel gehemmter Schüler. Zeitschrift angewandte Psychologie, 32:102–63 (1929).
126. ———. Psychodiagnostisches Praktikum. Eine Einführung in Hermann Rorschachs Formdeuteversuch. Barth, Leipzig, 1936.
127. Sender, Sadie, and B. Klopfer. Application of the Rorschach Test to child behavior problems as facilitated by a refinement of the scoring method. Rorschach Research Exchange, 1:5–17 (1936–37).
128. Sharp, S. E. Individual psychology. American Journal of Psychology, 10:329–91 (1899).
129. Shuey, H. A new interpretation of the Rorschach Test. Psychological Review, 40:213–15 (1933).
130. Sicha, K., and Mary Sicha. A step toward the standardization of the scoring of the Rorschach Test. Rorschach Research Exchange, 1:95–101 (1936–37).
131. Skalweit, W. Der Rorschach-Versuch als Unterscheidungsmittel von Konstitution und Prozess. Zeitschrift für die gesamte Neurologie und Psychiatrie, 152:605–10 (1935).
132. Snedecor, G. W. Statistical methods. Iowa State College Press, Ames, 1940.
133. Stavrianos, Bertha. An investigation of sex differences in children as revealed by the Rorschach method. Rorschach Research Exchange, 6:168–75 (1942).
134. Suares, Nadine. Personality development in adolescence. Rorschach Research Exchange, 3:2–11 (1938–39).
135. Sunne, Dagny. Rorschach Test norms of young children. Child Development, 7:304–13 (1936).
136. Terman, L. M., and Maud A. Merrill. Measuring intelligence. Houghton Mifflin, New York, 1937.
137. Thornton, G. R. A note on the scoring of movement in the Rorschach Test. American Journal of Psychology, 48:524–25 (1936).
138. Thornton, G. R., and J. P. Guilford. The reliability and meaning of Erlebnistypus scores in the Rorschach Test. Journal of Abnormal and Social Psychology, 31:324–30 (1936).
139. Treloar, A. E. Elements of statistical reasoning. John Wiley and Sons, New York, 1939.
140. Troup, Evelyn. A comparative study by means of the Rorschach method of personality development in 20 pairs of identical twins. Genetic Psychology Monograph, 20:461–556 (1938).
141. Troup, Evelyn, and B. Klopfer. Sample case studies. Rorschach Research Exchange, 1:121–40 (1936–37).

142. TULCHIN, S. H. The pre-Rorschach use of inkblot tests. Rorschach Research Exchange, 4:1–7 (1940).
143. UPDEGRAFF, RUTH. Recent approaches to the study of the preschool child. 1. Indirect and "projective" methods. Journal of Consulting Psychology, 2:159–61 (1938).
144. VAUGHN, J., and O. KRUG. The analytical character of the Rorschach Ink-Blot Test. American Journal of Orthopsychiatry, 8:220–29 (1938).
145. VERNON, P. E. The Rorschach Ink-Blot Test. British Journal of Medical Psychology, 13:89–118, 179–205, 271–95 (1933).
146. ———. Recent work on the Rorschach Test. Journal of Mental Science, 81:894–920 (1935).
147. ———. The significance of the Rorschach Test. British Journal of Medical Psychology, 15:199–217 (1935).
148. ———. Rorschach bibliography, Number III. Rorschach Research Exchange, 1:89–93 (1936–37).
149. VERSCHUER, O. V. Erbpsychologische Untersuchungen an Zwillingen. Zeitschrift induktive Abstammungs—und Vererbungslehre, 54:280–85 (1930).
150. VORHAUS, PAULINE G. Rorschach reactions in early childhood. Part III, Content and details in preschool records. Rorschach Research Exchange, 8:71–91 (1944).
151. WELLS, F. L. Rorschach and the free association test. Journal of Genetic Psychology, 13:413–33 (1935).
152. WERTHAM, F., and M. BLEULER. Inconstancy of the formal structure of the personality: experimental study of the influence of mescaline on the Rorschach Test. Archives of Neurology and Psychiatry, 28:52–70 (1932).
153. WHIPPLE, G. M. Manual of mental and physical tests. Warwick and York, Baltimore, 1924.
154. WHITE, R. Influence of suggestibility on responses in ink-blot tests. Child Development, 2:76–79 (1931).

INDEX

www.ingramcontent.com/pod-product-compliance
Ingram Content Group UK Ltd.
Pitfield, Milton Keynes, MK11 3LW, UK
UKHW020207290926
15470UKWH00001B/53

9 780837 158921